What people are saying about *Beyond Time Management...*

"Many books talk about discovery and formulation of purpose and vision, but this book really fleshes out the picture of living a life of purpose."—**Denis Murstein**, Director, Youth Network Council

"This book takes off where others leave off. It shows how to live powerfully by purpose day to day."—**Dag Tellefsen**, Founder and Managing Director, Glenwood International

"The final chapter on 'application of purpose in business' is worth tens of thousands of dollars in consulting for those who spend the time reading and reflecting. This book could save corporations big bucks in consulting fees and allow for better application of the dollars that are spent."—**Brian Laperriere**, Vice President, Bergos and Associates

"For me, this is the definitive book on living your purpose; it should be required reading for life."—**Don Moon**, President, Shimer College

"The power of purpose is presented with undeniable directness and simplicity. It helped me understand the concept much more deeply and presented a most significant inspiration and challenge. Now the job of persistence, courage and continued learning is up to me!"—**Michael Allen**, President, Banque Kleinwort Benson

"This book is the most detailed, practical book on 'purpose' I have read."—**Michael Zwell**, Ph.D., President, Zwell International

Beyond Time Management

Business with Purpose

ROBERT J. WRIGHT

Butterworth-Heinemann

Boston Oxford Johannesburg Melbourne New Delhi Singapore

Library of Congress Cataloging-in-Publication Data

Wright, Robert J.
    Beyond time management : business with purpose / Robert J. Wright.
        p.   cm.
    Includes index.
    ISBN 0-7506-9799-7 (pbk.)
    1. Management by objectives.   2. Goal setting in personnel
management.   3. Time management.   I. Title.
HD30.65.W75   1997
658.4'012—dc20   96-27816
                                                                    CIP

British Library Cataloguing-in-Publication Data
A catalogue record for this book is available from the British Library.

The publisher offers special discounts on bulk orders of this book.
For information, please contact:
Manager of Special Sales
Butterworth-Heinemann
313 Washington Street
Newton, MA 02158-1626
Tel: 617-928-2500
Fax: 617-928-2620

For information on all Business publications available, contact our World Wide Web home page at: http://www.bh.com/bb

10 9 8 7 6 5 4 3 2 1

Printed in the United States of America

Table of Contents

Acknowledgments

I want this book to be an acknowledgment of all that is finest in the human family. Unfortunately, for the sake of confidentiality, I cannot name those who most deserve to be named here. They are the many partners in living purpose who give me daily lessons and inspiration: my consulting and training clients. To them and other dear ones, who have contributed directly and indirectly to this effort, my deepest gratitude.

The one person most responsible for this effort is David Banner, who performed major surgery, piecing pieces together, and provided ideas, editing, and life support to keep the flame going until he brought the book to Karen Speerstra at Butterworth-Heinemann. He is a beloved covoyager and really a parent to this effort. Werner Erhard first introduced me to purpose as a powerful abstraction. Willie Cade coached me to learn to live it daily. Serita Stevens got the whole ball rolling, and Mary Thunder helped me get back on track.

Many staff have supported the effort over the years, but my business partner, Bob Kauffman, believed in me when I most needed it. Gordon Medlock has been midwife, baby-sitter, contributor, and occasional surgeon to the project. Lisa Yusk and Roger Patience worked tirelessly on editing and typing. Spiritual guides Jim Morningstar and Vicki Schuver have helped me stay clear on my highest purpose with advice, comfort, and, most of all, their exemplary lives.

Last and most important is my partner in life, my heroine in dedication and devotion, my comfort in fear and hurt, my example of constant appreciation of all that is good and decent in others, Judith Ellen Sewell Wright, my loving wife. Being around Judith is to be around one who lives her purpose impeccably.

Introduction

I have had the honor over the last twenty years to coach some of the most remarkably dedicated, caring people imaginable—people committed to manifesting their highest with the courage to face and deal with their darkest. This book is ostensibly about peak accomplishment through purpose, but it is really about them and their commitment to personal development, service, and, ultimately, love. I only hope I have demonstrated their magnificence adequately as I describe their struggles to bring their dreams to reality in business and the rest of their lives.

The pursuit of their dreams draws them forward into the fullest production and satisfaction imaginable. The power of living their deepest vision fills them with desire that causes them to find ways to do things others would think impossible. On the surface, some of their accomplishments may seem ordinary unless we understand the magnitude of the barriers they faced on their individual paths to their ultimate. The life of purpose is an individual one that defies comparison but invites appreciation and fellow voyagers.

I met most of these inspiring individuals through my consulting and coaching practice after I quit doing traditional training in sales, communications, teamwork, and other performance-enhancement activities. We had the good fortune to see explosions such as sales districts increasing their position in a field of 2000 from 200 to 16 after one month of coaching at midyear. Unfortunately, I also watched the crash-and-burn phenomenon that happened to so many after an inspiring seminar and initially exciting results. I quit doing work for the U. S. Army and some of the largest insurance, printing, and pharmaceutical companies in the world to focus on more lasting, meaningful change.

I began working for what I call ideologically driven companies, headed by individuals willing to declare the ideals for which they stand and be rated on and held accountable to these by their employees and clients or customers. This immediately led to a drop in the size of my client companies and a significant rise in my satisfaction and the results we achieved. Rather than delivering seminars, I was coaching dedicated individuals on living to their highest. They, in turn, became "walking seminars," transforming their companies from the inside. Starting with internal transformation personally, they created more honest, inclusive, inspirational work teams and companies.

"Beyond time management" became a focus for me in the early 1980s, when I was commissioned by Robert Oaks Jordan to develop an anti-procrastination program for the U.S. Army at Ft. Sheridan, Illinois. He had been receiving a great number of requests for time management training by the top officers at the fort. Ever the perceptive observer, Bob questioned the need and proceeded to do a study on the subject at the facility. He found that the problem was not a lack of time management knowledge: the officers were conversant in the techniques and ways of accomplishment. Despite their knowledge, many failed to perform anywhere near their potential. It was this discovery that led Jordan to conclude that the real need was to deal with procrastination, as a result of which the PAY Game, Procrastination Appreciation for You, was developed. This one-week seminar with weekly reinforcement sessions over the next three months was the first place outside our company where I began experimenting with the power of purpose.

Central to the concepts of procrastination and performance was the simple reality that people get things done when they must. Similarly, people who are going somewhere do what they need to do to get there, and people who aren't, don't. To learn to live with a sense of purpose is to be going toward the most important, compelling destination possible for any of us. When we do this we are assertively following our destiny, and the forces around us seem to line up to cheer us on as we initiate facing our fiercest foes without waiting for circumstances to force us.

It is no simple feat to face our eventualities before they rush in on us in force. Without purpose, it's as if destiny begins to call us with a gentle tap on the shoulder. If we respond, fine. If we fail to respond, the tap becomes increasingly forceful, until we are thrown to the ground. With a clear sense of purpose, we are more likely to be sensitive to the earlier taps and address the needs around us in a more timely fashion.

That is the general approach to moving beyond time management we address in this book. Time management courses are always a good idea. In preparation for the Ft. Sheridan job, I attended as many as I could and found that rules of time management, such as "touch things only once" and "work expands to fill time" are really useful. Before, during, and after the program I even hired a productivity coach. For four months I religiously wrote and kept score of my accomplishment of daily priorities, phoning in my results at the end of each day. My time in productivity coaching extended to almost two years of regular meetings and review.

Nothing I learned was as important and compelling as the concept and reality of *purpose*. With clear purpose, things fit better, and my fire seemed to burn brighter. The fire was contagious. Our company grew by leaps and bounds as we became stronger in our purpose. Our staff and clients operated with zeal and inspiration. Then, after eight years, we grew too fast. Our first major staff conflict and turnover took place, and I lost my clarity of purpose. The next five years were filled with uncertainty and agony as I wandered in the dark, seeing no further than the purpose of keeping the company together.

I knew what my problem was but could not convincingly rekindle the flame I had lost. I even led seminars on "purpose," hoping no one would ask me for mine. When they did and I told them I was unclear at the moment, it was painful and embarrassing. I couldn't fake it, because my purpose had seemed like a sacred beacon I did not want to desecrate. In my quest to become reoriented, I attended retreats and seminars. Finally on a Native American vision quest, I once again found a clear sense of and statement of purpose that has guided me since. It sits clipped to a panel in my briefcase, where I see it every day. When I need to make difficult decisions, when I want to find the right idea from a number of good ideas, I look at it, and weigh my alternatives against it to see which is most attuned, and go on from there.

At its finest, a clear statement of purpose is a reflection of our essence. By attuning to it we are drawn on the worthiest, most exciting, most fulfilling quest we can engage in. Enhancing performance is a by-product of this quest.

Most of us find the statement of purpose too abstract for daily application. To make purpose more immediately accessible, we present the principles of purpose for individuals and corporations. These could also be called the principles of accomplishment, because they help us to our highest performance, with or without clarity of purpose. By learning to live in consonance with these principles, we automatically live close to the centerline of our purpose and accomplish more as we develop our capacities to their highest. Living true to the principles compels toward more fulfilling, better and faster living while at the same time providing more meaning and technical vehicles that move us powerfully forward.

I hope this book will help you discover the added joy and power of a life of clear, conscious purpose, and if you are already operating with a clear sense of purpose, I hope this reminder and elaboration will make your journey richer, lighter, and more energized.

Bob Wright
May 15, 1996

Part 1

Principles of Purpose

Chapter 1

A Tale of Time Management

Challenging the meaning of life . . . is the truest expression of the state of being human.

...VIKTOR FRANKL

Once upon a time there was a man named John who wanted ever so badly to be a good person and to "get ahead." He took courses on personal productivity and assertiveness. He learned that he should listen more, so he took courses on how to listen. He was told that time was his most valuable resource and that he should learn to manage it better. He began taking courses on time management. The courses taught him many useful techniques, but slowly John became aware that it is impossible to "manage" time. Time simply is; it cannot be administered or trained, which is what the word "manage" means. He could manage his work-flow, his staff, or his projects, but he couldn't manage time. He started to see time instead as the playing field on which he operated his business and personal affairs. Like the boundary and yard lines in the football field: it defines the limits of play.

He played the game to get as much high-quality work done "within the lines" as possible; his budget, his staff, his own efforts, and his customers were for him like teams on the playing field, and he developed winning game plans to bring them all to success.

John's resource management and mastery of time helped him prosper. He learned many useful planning and maximizing techniques: handling papers only once, prioritizing and setting goals, charting and planning projects years in advance. He mastered all these techniques, and he taught his staff to do the same. Rising in his company, with an exceptional salary, he still felt he had barely tapped his potential. The nagging question remained: "What's it all about, anyway? Why do I do these things?" His old answer, "To get ahead," was no longer satisfying and was replaced by the dangerous, unfulfilling answer so many workers and executives at all levels tell themselves: "For my family, my spouse, and the children." The problem with this reasoning is that personal fulfillment is "sacrificed" for family. Naturally the worker is eventually in some way unhappy, and finally doesn't bring his or her best back to the family, and all suffer.

One spring, less than a year after his latest promotion—to executive vice president in charge of sales and marketing—John found himself unusually perplexed. This was supposed to be the point where everything came out right. His children were grown and graduated from college, the house was paid for, and he'd traveled around the world with his wife, yet the same nagging question arose: "Why?" There was something missing. He was good at his job, yet he yearned for more. He was certain he hadn't come anywhere close to tapping his potential. He went back to the time management and other business consultants he had used over the years, and they all said he needed a new goal. This didn't seem quite right. He was one step from president of the company and was sure that step wouldn't make any real difference. He could see the top, and there was nothing significantly different.

In frustration, he decided the answer would have to come from himself. So he told his staff he'd be gone indefinitely, flew to Denver, rented a car, and headed for the mountains, with no particular destination in mind. He found a secluded, privately run hotel and conference center at the top of a pass, with spectacular views from every room. He felt comfortable in the large,

Ralph Lauren style building with its natural log walls and ceiling. The lodge was decorated with Native American weavings and overstuffed furniture and had plenty of nooks and crannies for him to hide out in and read when he wasn't hiking in the mountain meadows among the wildflowers. He sweated in the sauna and swam in the heated outdoor pool of this exclusive hideaway, asking himself what was missing. He was sure the grandeur of the vistas and vital force of the springtime swollen mountain streams would help him get his head clear, if anything could.

The staff was friendly and he enjoyed the break, but after the first two and a half days he seemed no closer to an answer. On the third morning, after breakfast, he went to the library, where an old man was straightening the room. He was dressed in a flannel work shirt and worn blue jeans. John figured he must be some retired fellow who couldn't get by on his pension and worked here as a janitor to make ends meet.

"Are you here for the sales seminar?" asked the man as he put some books away.

"No," John answered, "I'm just here to think."

"What are you thinking about?" he questioned as he straightened the magazines. "If you don't mind me asking."

"Oh, just about what's missing," answered John.

"Whadd'ya mean?" asked the old man casually.

"Well," said John, and he launched into his story.

The older man listened with interest, asking questions about John's career and life. He seemed like a nice person, and John was surprised at how easily he talked to this stranger about things he felt so deeply but had thought about so little. He discussed his early transition from personnel into sales when he realized that a staff position would never get him to what he viewed as a position of real importance. He talked about his love of the teams he had led.

John thought about other decisions that had changed his life, like when he took the new job at the billion-dollar fast-growing Crowley because being director of sales for a fifteen-million-dollar family-owned company was never going to make him really happy. The story went on and on. John became self-conscious at several points. The old man said it sounded like his own life and that he was enjoying reminiscing too. As the sun set, Herb, who had revealed his name during the conversation, sent John off to a bittersweet dinner reflecting on some new angles.

John began thinking about the times he had moved to get ahead and wondered what would have happened if he'd just stayed where he was. His wife was usually upset at the changes but got over it quickly as they moved from one big challenge to the next. He wondered what her life would have been like if they hadn't left Boston, where her design business was taking off. She'd even been getting national attention with several awards and national magazine exposure. He went to bed with a strange mixture of sadness, longing, and satisfaction that he couldn't put into a neat package.

The next morning he felt wonderfully refreshed as he hurried through breakfast to catch the early raft trip Herb had told him about down the Green River. He'd never been on a white-water river before and the combination of breathtaking scenery and danger held his absolute attention the entire day. Once back, he was awed by the images that continued to course through his mind: sheer cliffs, deer grazing, the deep green of the mountain meadows, and the trees that seemed to absorb his worries. The floor seemed to be undulating as if he were still swaying in the raft. He felt he had been transported into another world, and he longed to be with his wife and children to share it all . He called home, said goodnight to everyone, and went to the reading room to write a postcard to his staff. He felt really good for the first time since he had arrived.

Herb was standing talking to the receptionist when John went to the desk to buy some stamps. They got to talking about his day, and John asked Herb if he would like to join him for a late dinner. Herb accepted the invitation and went to make a phone call, saying he'd see John in fifteen minutes. The conversation was about the Green River and other Colorado wonders Herb loved so deeply. Herb turned out to be the owner of the lodge, hardly the laborer John had imagined. He had built a substantial ad agency in New York and sold it at retirement a few years before to build this place. John was shocked—Herb hardly seemed like the hard-driving ad execs he'd dealt with in the past.

John was impressed by Herb's straightforward perspective on business and people and talked further about what had brought him to the lodge. He asked for Herb's thoughts. The answer surprised him.

"It's simple . . . you have all the right tools and you've made all the right moves, but you haven't clarified your purpose!"

"What do you mean?" asked John, feeling skeptical and puzzled. "Are you getting mystical or something with me?"

"Heck no, it's just as plain as the nose on your face. There's no mystery," replied an amused Herb.

"If there's no mystery, how come I understood everything you said until now except this?" challenged John. He was becoming annoyed with the direction of the conversation.

"You don't understand what I'm saying because you've become too smart. Now that's okay—it's how you've succeeded until now. I can tell you're a good man and that you're dependable, but you look at things backwards. You consider looking inward a waste of time, and for such a caring man, you live your life with almost no heart."

John knew Herb was right, but he resented his statements all the same, and it was all he could do to keep listening.

Herb continued, "You do what you do without knowing why. That makes everything harder. Take me, for example. I work more hours per week and enjoy myself even more now than I did at the agency. I'm here to serve people like you. I provide a space to plan your heart's desire. I cheer people up when they're down. I get people out of a funk in nothing flat. Serving fully fills me so my long days nourish me better than most peoples' vacations do for them."

"That's easy for you to say, but I've got demands on me that don't lend themselves to such easy answers," replied John defensively. He knew he was wrong, but he thought Herb couldn't possibly understand the demands of *his* life.

"Oh, sure you do," replied the older man gently. "That's all the more reason you need to be really honest with yourself."

"What do you mean, 'honest with myself'?" challenged John.

"How important is your work, really? How satisfied and fulfilled are you each day as you make plans and impress everyone? Do you feel you're making the difference in your own and others' lives that you really want, down deep? Are your and others' lives enriched spiritually as well as materially?

"Let's say you've got four things to do and they're all important. Which one are you gonna do?"

"Why, the one that's the highest priority!" replied John.

"Okay, but what's the highest priority, and who picks your priorities?"

"Why, I do."

"Are you sure? Are you really in charge, or do the things around you run you?"

"Look, I've done plenty of time management seminars, and I do a pretty good job of managing things. I know how to set goals and priorities."

"Sure you do, but what are you doing here, then?"

"Well, I'm beginning to see your point. Are you saying there are some priorities I'm missing?"

"I guess you could say that. If we use your language, I'd say you're missing the one priority from which all the others flow. You just aren't clear on what you're here for. You've been learning to do all kinds of things without knowing why, really. You've used excuses to get ahead—not the deepest, most meaningful criteria for your decisions. That's okay—it's all part of growing up. You've just done it the hard way, like most of us."

"What do you mean?"

"I did the same thing you did. It was only when my wife died that I began reading and studying and learning to feel deeply enough to find out what I'm here for. When she died, I went into a deep depression. I didn't feel I had a reason to live. I thought I needed to find it again but learned I'd never really known it in the first place. Eventually, the agency became a joyful playground for serving and learning. The staff really pulled together but we faced a lot of barriers to get there. The struggle was hard for me, but it doesn't have to be so painful for you if you get going now. You've got all the pieces in place, as far as I can tell. You just haven't discovered the 'why' and learned to live it."

"That sounds good, but I'm still not sure what you're getting at," pursued John.

"You don't know your purpose, and you've learned how to do things without understanding how life works! They didn't give us a manual when we were born. That's part of the game. We learn the rules by trial and error. Cocky people like you and me are the thickest-headed."

"Oh really!" quipped John.

"Yeah. You see, I know why I'm here and what I'm doing. I've got purpose. You've got purpose, too, but your head isn't clear on it. Everyone has it in their heart. But since you're uncertain, you're always somewhat divided—your heart isn't totally behind what you do. It can't put its full power into your activities until you've aligned your goals with your deepest yearnings. Your goals are hollow without purpose to give them meaning. They won't bring your life into a harmonious whole.

"When you're purposeful in what you do, you're in charge, even when you let someone else lead. You see, we humans have forgotten our dignity, and we bounce around 'reacting' to the world instead of 'creating' our world. You're better than most, but you still need to get to the essence of what you're really about."

"That sounds pretty abstract. How do we do it?" asked John.

"By asking the right questions and really listening for the answers, whether we like them or not. Asking the right questions is an art. A most useful question is the one you came with: 'What am I here for, or what is my purpose, and how do I get on with it the best way possible and avoid the distractions?' It's as simple as that! Fulfillment and all you've worked so hard for will follow."

"Yeah, sounds simple as you say it, but where do I start? How do I discover my purpose?"

The rest of the book reveals what John discovered on his journey as he set about working and living with a conscious purpose.

Chapter 2

The Power of Purpose

This is the true joy in life: The being used for a purpose recognized by yourself as a mighty one. The being a force of nature rather than a feverish, selfish clod of ailments and grievances complaining that the world will not devote itself to making you happy.

...George Bernard Shaw

This book is about the opportunity, challenge, and responsibility each of us has every moment of every day to live fulfilled lives; learning, growing, and full of meaning. From this perspective, accomplishment is seen as a by-product of fulfilling our potential and our heart's desire. Too often, most of us wait to accomplish things to be fulfilled rather than experiencing fulfillment in every moment and in every situation. With purpose, we see greater possibility in every situation and stop waiting to live and love, because we are living and loving our fullest toward our highest, honoring life in all its manifestations.

In the following pages you will have an opportunity to learn about the nature of purpose and its principles. You will develop your vision for increasing your life effectiveness and fulfillment by learning to live a consciously purposeful existence. You will see numerous examples of how we fulfill our potential by fulfilling our heart's desire.

You will meet people, or composites of people, who are living lives of purpose, people who overcome great obstacles on their way to their highest. Most of them have dedicated a good deal of effort to their personal growth and life effectiveness. Most names, occupations, and, in some cases, sexes have been changed to honor their confidentiality, but the stories are theirs and the inspiration from them. Any failure to engage you, the reader, is a result of my shortcomings as a storyteller. My excitement and reward, participating with them on their journeys to personal fulfillment and community service, cannot be exaggerated.

Each of their stories is an opportunity for you to contact your highest self—to see your full potential and know you are in good company on the ultimate, lifelong adventure: higher-purpose fulfillment.

WHAT IS PURPOSE?

Purpose refers to a wonderful capacity in each of us—to joyously take our place in the progress of humanity and do our part to help all reach full potential. Purpose is the heart of the matter, the "why" behind what we do. It summarizes our reason for doing what we are doing. A clear life purpose gives meaning to all activities. Life purpose is the container into which we fit our goals. If we think of a projector shining a concentrated light through film onto a screen, purpose is the lens through which life flows to project our highest vision.

John found a most important secret of life when he took Herb's advice. His life journey became more challenging. He began accomplishing and learning more than he had previously imagined possible. His sense of purpose evolved as he developed beyond his wildest dreams. It was as if he had found a long-lost friend: himself. His highest self was emerging.

As he lived his purpose, he kept on course by living the principles of purpose, aliveness, play, intention, truth, commitment, and responsibility. With them, he found ways of accomplishment and power beyond goal setting and time management, ways that increase both effectiveness and fulfillment. He found that purpose provided the focus for the fulfillment of his heart's desires, which automatically led to even greater accomplishment. His goals became more compelling. He accomplished them more quickly with purpose, the source from which goal setting and time management flow. He increased his power. The principles of purpose led him to engage more fully and drew him into communication he would otherwise have avoided. They marshaled his forces and aligned him with the greater good. A clearer life-vision emanated from his purpose and guided him. As he communicated his vision, he inspired others. John was on fire with desire and meaning, and so were his staff. This drive carried them through troubling times where they would have stalled in the past. They were still challenged but had discovered a key tool to help them face life's ever present challenges. Their life journey was even sometimes harder and more frustrating but it was always more rewarding.

Living with purpose increased their fulfillment, because they focused on the most essential good for themselves and the company. By focusing on their highest good and the greater good for all, they became increasingly "in tune" internally. Harmony resulted, and their actions increasingly flowed from their deepest concerns. The well-being of other employees, customers, and community became the beacon by which they guided their ship. Let's explore how John went about starting this fire of passionate performance in himself and his staff.

In identifying his life purpose, John looked ahead to the end of his life. He identified the things he liked doing, was best at, and that had the most meaning for him. Putting these together, he discovered that his career was a perfect vehicle for his life purpose. It led to his fullest, most unique contribution. He saw his purpose as developing his personal gifts: learning, growing, and serving, so that his family, friends, coworkers, and customers could live the highest quality of life possible.

John learned to use his life purpose like a touchstone in daily decisions. He found he could see to the heart of matters more easily. He shifted from managing detail to managing process. Work flowed more freely, and his enjoyment increased dramatically. As he stopped worrying about details, he began experiencing the power of aiming at higher targets.

He delegated more effectively and became a better trainer and supervisor. He allowed those who reported to him more freedom, because he was focused on their ultimate development and success. He let go of control but increased his responsibility. His staff responded with even greater productivity and creativity. Purposeful action meant fewer errors. Work became easier for them all as he taught them to operate "on purpose." He felt greater fulfillment and creativity because he was no longer bogged down in details. His staff became a source of constant support, excitement, and fulfillment. In the tough times they worked through conflicts and problems more effectively, teaching John more than he had imagined possible. Fear and pain were more easily overcome with a good reason to face them.

John's family life benefited too. His family became more than just people to support. They became a more integrated part of his daily life. John was more aware than ever of the importance of his role with his children. He discovered a richness in contributing to them he had missed in the past. He and his wife came to see each other more fully as partners with complementary skills, exploring the richness of common purpose. Expecting more and more of each other, they found great fulfillment and intimacy, even as they found themselves fighting more often. These conflicts resolved in an ever-deepening sense of mutual understanding, alignment, and growth, making the conflict an inconsequential part of a much larger journey. Past hurts were healed and less was swept under the rug.

John no longer felt as though he lived in completely separate worlds of work and family. His life had become an integrated whole. He felt uplifted by his work as well as his leisure and family life. He'd always been excited and challenged, but now he was inspired. John's children felt more comfortable with him as he relaxed more with them. John's staff began talking about the "newer, kinder John." He got more done and experienced less friction. His creativity blossomed as he focused on where he was going—and why—rather than following rigid plans.

He found he had more energy than ever before. He ran for and was elected to the school board, where, with his ability to see the big picture, he soon became president. Because of his greater perspective, he could find the common elements in conflicting issues and arrive at creative, win-win solutions for administrators, teachers, students, and the community.

John's daily discipline included measuring decisions and actions against his higher purpose and following the principles of purpose—an adventure that both tuned him in and turned him on. His inspiration excited those around him as well. He cherished the journey and what he was experiencing. He'd gone from successful to fulfilled.

Each one of us has an overarching life purpose or reason for being. Sometimes we can boil this down into a purpose statement; sometimes it remains an unstated, motivating force that directs our actions. A well-articulated, accurate life-purpose statement brings our highest goals and principles into focus in a way that helps us clarify choices and move forward. It provides the foundation for powerful, integrated vision. It serves as the ultimate guide to balance in our lives. As we sort our way through life choices, we can keep our purpose in mind to more easily identify which alternative best forwards our ultimate aim. It helps us make stronger, more deliberate choices while indicating where to let go of unproductive directions and move on to places where our talents are best used.

PURPOSE AND GOALS

Purpose provides the why; goals are the what. Without purpose, goals lack meaning. Purpose defines goals the way a bowl defines a serving of strawberries. Without the bowl, the strawberries are scattered, unrelated. Without purpose, goals lack coherence, order, direction, and power.

Many of us know the disappointment of achieving a goal and discovering that the good feelings and satisfaction we expected just disappeared. We graduate, and life is not what we imagined. We get married, and our lives don't turn out to be the romance we dreamed of. We get the new job, and we discover that the new challenges are harder than we ever thought.

Purpose

Figure 2.1

UNITY OF MEANING AND ACTIONS

With purpose, achieving goals is more fulfilling, because we can more readily sense the larger meaning and journey into which the goals fit. Employees who work within a context of clear purpose are more likely to joyously engage in mundane tasks. Window cleaning is not just a chore but an important part of the entire company purpose. There is a better reason to do the windows than "the boss wants me to." I want to because I am engaged in the company purpose. Each small goal is a part of the whole.

At the auto dealership where I bought my last car, everyone from the porters to the owner engages in his or her tasks with enthusiasm. The shop is spotless to show off the wonderful vehicles, the porters proudly sweep the shop floor or open a car door, and the salespeople sound like adoring sports fans when they talk about the engineering that goes into the cars. For this company, sales goals, service goals, and other maintenance goals all fit into the higher purpose of adding to the quality of customers' lives by providing an effective, uplifting driving experience.

Throughout this book you will encounter AMPs. This stands for Appreciating My Purpose or Assessment and Monitoring of

Purpose. They give you the opportunity to pause and reflect on your own experience so you can deepen your understanding and apply the material.

If we lack unity of purpose, goals become fragmented and lose meaning. The company loses power and fulfillment is diminished. Frustration increases, and we find it more difficult to sort our way through the rough times. **(AMP)***

Searle, the pharmaceutical company, was founded by G.D. Searle. He had a mission to promote healing through what he called ethical pharmaceuticals. This quest led to the discovery of the birth control pill. The pill led to such windfall profits that his sons, who were then running the company, found themselves with one of the most profitable companies in the world per capital dollar invested.

They used the windfall profits as so many do—to diversify and expand their empire. Rather than remaining focused on the company purpose of promoting health through ethical pharmaceuticals, they bought health-related companies left and right in far-flung, diverse activities. The end result was a multi-faceted empire of companies without unity of purpose. Many divisions and products never quite took off. Others were second to the market with product breakthroughs. Company goals were no longer unified by a common higher purpose, and research lost focus and direction. The company floundered so badly that a professional manager was brought in to divest the company of tangential and unprofitable divisions. His job was to prepare the company for sale.

Searle had watered down its power and effectiveness because it lacked a coherent purpose.

---

* AMP—Think of a situation where goal accomplishment was not as fulfilling as you or someone else had hoped. Why do you think this was so? Think of a time when goals lacked coherence and meaning. What did it feel like?

PURPOSE INCREASES POWER
AND AVOIDS BURNOUT

I want to be thoroughly used up when I die . . . for the harder I work the more I live. I rejoice in life for its own sake. Life is no brief candle for me. It is sort of a splendid torch.

...GEORGE BERNARD SHAW

Not only do people with a clear sense of purpose move through life with greater ease, grace, and power. They accomplish goals faster and with less effort while others look on in envy. They experience much less burnout. Too often, we mistakenly believe that accomplishment and suffering go together. Nothing could be further from the truth. In our most joyful, engaged states, we accomplish the most. We are enlivened, not drained. We accomplish more because, when we have purpose, our goals take on more meaning. With more meaning, we are more fully engaged. We are more conscious and less ambivalent. It is not overwork but ambivalence and low fulfillment that cause burnout. The most fulfilled people move to purpose fulfillment the way a plant is drawn to the sun. They experience power, not drain.

Purpose enhances power because we can more fully give ourselves to what we do. When we give ourselves fully, resistance is minimized and we are drawn forward as if a magnet were pulling us rapidly to our destiny. Purpose frees our productivity. With it, we can take our foot off the brake and drive as fast as our heart desires. At other times, it provides the guidance we need to carefully pick our way through the debris of disaster.

When we are uncertain or lost, purpose acts like a compass to orient us or a beacon toward which we are drawn. Like an internal gyroscope, it keeps us upright in the storm. A clear sense of purpose guides chief executives and cab drivers alike. Doormen see the part they can play in providing an uplifting tone in people's day, and office workers feel the satisfaction of serving both clients and coworkers.

Self-maintenance, not burnout, is necessary for the highest fulfillment of this joyous aim. To perform in our work at a world-class level and sustain this, we must refresh ourselves with similar world-class skill. This includes high-quality rest as well as high return of fulfillment from our employment investment. Mutual nourishment comes when we serve each other from the perspective of our highest purpose. When we do this, we are more likely to move through pain and disappointment together and experience the support of others as we take our part in the positive development of humanity.

ENHANCED PERFORMANCE

Purpose not only gives form and meaning to goals, it helps get work done faster, more easily, with more fulfillment, and in a more integrated way. Most of us wait to go to the doctor as long as we can. We tend to put things off until it is absolutely necessary to attend to them. When we do this, we act more to avoid problems than to accomplish goals and, certainly not to fulfill our purpose.

Applied daily, a clear sense of purpose spurs us to get things done. We act to produce an important result rather than avoid problems. We've all seen the results of people pulling together in the face of natural disasters such as floods and hurricanes. Purpose can motivate us, even without impending disaster, by helping us attune to our heart's desires. We can feel the natural delight of generation and communication. Purpose delivers a compelling call to a higher good. We develop an urgency to serve. What we do takes on more importance, and we perform to higher levels with more satisfaction than we thought imaginable.

Ellis

The man I am going to describe provides a most inspirational example for me. He serves without burnout, orients to higher purpose in times of confusion, and has discovered the powerful motivation of following higher purpose by orienting to his heart's desire. Ellis, a consultant, exemplifies enhanced performance through a clear sense of purpose. This wasn't always the case for him. From early on, Ellis wanted to be well known and make a lot of money. This was his highest conscious purpose for many years. He lived in a feast-or-famine world. To make ends meet, he even once traded his house for a less expensive one. His life was dominated by fear and chaos. He began living by the principles of purpose, and then his career purpose took form. Over the years he discovered the joy of partnering with his clients in fulfilling their dreams. His sense of purpose expanded. As money receded in importance, he made more. As fame became irrelevant, he was mentioned more and more. He became absorbed in meeting his clients' needs. In so doing, his own needs were met or exceeded. His famine periods receded, and life became remarkably enjoyable.

When he moved from a limited purpose of making money and becoming famous to one of serving clients and fully helping them succeed, he discovered unanticipated excitement. This enthusiasm caused him to conceptualize and develop new products at breakneck speed. He wanted to serve as much as possible. Clarity of purpose helped him prioritize product development and keep focused on the well-being of his growing organization. He even split off a major portion of his business because the key executives were not in line with his higher purpose.

His upbeat attitude was contagious. His staff began producing at higher levels than they had ever imagined possible. They had more products than ever but experienced a unity of purpose and direction that caused them to feel more focused and purposeful than ever before. They knew that people were lucky to do business with them, and they were grateful to have those clients to serve. They could afford to decline inappropriate business because their thirst and hunger were quenched by their purposeful alignment. They engaged in work wholeheartedly and were always looking for ways to do things better, to leverage themselves. Their efficiency was always improving, and innovative time- and energy-saving techniques became a matter of pride for all as they redefined their parameters of excellence.

Work had become a joy at Ellis's firm. By the end of January 1995, he had personally met ninety percent of his annual sales goals which were already doubled from the prior year. He was over one-hundred percent by the end of the first quarter. He had not experienced a down year in his last three. Just as some runners can cover a distance much faster than others, his firm had developed world-class creativity, productivity, and turn-around. They hardly noticed the extra time invested, because the fulfillment was so rewarding. **(AMP)***

Living with purpose is a skill that requires daily practice to develop. What is really impressive about Ellis is not his discovery of purpose but his discipline in applying his purpose and living the principles of purpose daily. He keeps himself on course with regular seminars and coaching and by serving as mentor and trainer to numerous others. His entire client/employee/family world benefits from his continual learning and growing in living true to his highest self.

PERSON-TO-PERSON PURPOSE

Purpose can be very focused on our immediate circumstances. It does not begin on a corporate or global scale. It begins with each individual and expands.

In January 1996, my wife entered a Chicago cab. The driver was Asian, and she had a difficult time understanding him at first. Finally she made out his question: "What you afraid of?" The unusual nature of the encounter and the depth of the question caused her to hesitate and reflect.

She responded, "I guess my biggest fear is that I won't do enough to love God in this lifetime."

"Well, at least you humble," he responded. "Everybody afraid of something—fear blocks love. Me, I afraid of my lust for women. It keeps me from Christ. People afraid. Beautiful women afraid to lose their beauty. Rich man afraid he lose his money. I ask Jesus to clean me of my dirty mind. It is too much for me, but not for him."

---

* AMP—Remember a time when your work felt important or urgent and your productivity skyrocketed. What were the circumstances? What did you feel? If you can't remember, ask others for examples.

The conversation continued along this vein for five minutes. The cabdriver seemed to be certain of his purpose, personally and in society. My wife was challenged and inspired. He had provided a call to consciousness. He was striving for a world in which we become more conscious and choose more conscious lives run by love, not fear, one encounter at a time. **(AMP)***

PURPOSE ENHANCES FLOW

Mihaly Csikszentmihalyi, in his book *Flow: The Psychology of Optimal Experience,* speaks of "the positive aspects of human experience—joy, creativity, the process of total involvement with life—the state in which people are so involved in an activity that nothing else seems to matter; the experience itself is so enjoyable that people will do it even at great cost, for the sheer sake of doing it."

Purpose enhances the experience of flow, adding impetus, direction, and meaning to what we do. We more easily accomplish our goals, because we are headed well beyond them. A major challenge in skiing, for example, is traversing a mogul field. These moguls, or bumps, ranging up to seven or eight feet high, represent obstacles. The novice skier fearfully skis from one bump to the next with no thought other than getting down the mountain unharmed. The more advanced skier picks a course through the bumps and does well until a surprise makes his or her original course impossible. He or she stops and starts again.

The expert skier picks a line and fluidly skis that line. Expert skiers seem to float over the moguls with a relatively still upper body and very busy pistonlike action in their legs. They keep oriented to their chosen line and their quick-turning skis seem to automatically pick the best path through the moguls.

---

* AMP—Think of people in your life who seem to live a clear sense of higher purpose. Reflect on the positive aspects of their lives. What are the aspects of their lives that give you the impression that they live a life of purpose? In what ways are you like them, and how would you like to be more like them?

Purpose enhances flow in life the way a line gives the expert skier a way of orientation. We flow smoothly through life's bumps as we engage actively and completely in daily life, gracefully flowing, working fully, like the legs of the advanced skier. Goals and barriers in life are like the moguls. Purpose provides the line. It is as if we are pulled through. We seem to flow. The resistance of the bumps becomes less important because we are aiming beyond them, at bigger things. We are aware of the bumps, we respect them, but do not preoccupy ourselves with them.

People with a clear sense of purpose linger less. They know where they are going and why. They are less likely to be stopped. In American football, each offensive play is designed to produce a touchdown. Ask any NFL runner if he imagines just running up to his tacklers. He will tell you he imagines running beyond them. This is the way of maximum forward momentum. He is much more likely to go a long way when he is aiming further.

Just as the runner sometimes breaks free for a long run, the worker with a greater sense of purpose is more likely to experience the flow of getting a great deal done. The worker without a great sense of purpose will more likely experience barriers as insurmountable and find more stasis and much less flow. We once had two workers who represented the dynamics of flow and stasis in the extreme. Carl was a strapping young man with an IQ in the top one percent. He considered himself a practicing Christian but did not integrate this into his work. If he left a message, he thought that ended his responsibility in setting up appointments. He did not follow through, but put things off as an inconvenience. Work was an imposition, and each barrier a stopping point. He experienced very little flow, and his worklife was a logjam.

Todd, on the other hand, saw his purpose in life as learning, growing, and making things work. His natural talents were meager compared to Carl's, but he loved to serve, and anything that needed doing was an opportunity. Where Carl stopped, Todd pushed; where Carl experienced breakdown, Todd experienced challenge. Todd's day had numerous instances of flow, while Carl experienced much less.

As Todd pushed through one barrier, he had momentum to accomplish the next more easily. He experienced the joy, excitement, and fulfillment of flow, while Carl experienced the heaviness of burden and felt overwhelmed. Carl had no guiding sense of purpose to his work, while Todd was purpose in action. Today, Todd is a consultant helping others succeed in business. He earns five times the hourly rate Carl commands in his new job.

Purpose enhances flow by allowing greater involvement. Greater involvement turns into greater focus through the lens of higher purpose, and the momentum of involvement translates to accomplishment and ultimately more instances of flow—the fulfillment available moment-by-moment, day-by-day, to all of us all the time, if we can only access it. **(AMP)***

PURPOSE ENHANCES CREATIVITY

> *The bigger the goal, the bigger the dream, the greater the creativity.*
>
> ...GALE GRIMMENGA

When we know why we are doing what we are doing, we can think more creatively. We can scan the world and match potential associations and courses of action against our purposes. Purpose helps us leave habit and move into the newness that spawns creativity. We spend an enormous part of our lives mired in habitual behavior. We seek the security of sameness to avoid the uncertainty of newness. We'll even cling to the same old pain rather than seek new pleasures—because of the perceived risk.

Paul Coelho, in his book *The Valkyries*, tells a story of training elephants. When the elephants are babies, they are chained

---

* AMP 1—Record moments of flow experiences in your life. Include examples from your work and your personal life. Ask others about flow in their lives.

* AMP 2—How did each experience contribute to the quality of your or others' lives?

to a log they cannot move. They try to escape, but the log is too heavy for them. Their memory of the immovable log attached to the chain is strong. Even after they grow to full size and could easily move the log, all the trainer needs to do is put the chain on their legs and they stand still. He can affix the chain to anything, even a twig, and they will remain where he leaves them. Our lives are similarly limited. We stop moving because we are unaware of our expanded capacities, just like the elephants. This habitual sameness limits our creative capacities significantly.

Purpose gives us something toward which we move, a compelling force that can break us out of the mold of our habits. We've all heard that necessity is the mother of invention. Purpose works the same way. Purpose necessitates movement, engendering the need for creativity. We walk away with the chains on. Our mind stretches to become more creative, recombining possibilities in new ways to further our purpose.

With purpose, there is flexibility—many goals can arise to meet our ultimate end. Flexibility allows us to see opportunities we might otherwise miss. We are freer to relate fully to the world in the here and now—by doing so, we unleash the creative power of our unconscious mind to solve problems. **(AMP)***

INDIVIDUAL CREATIVITY

Kristen had a Ph.D. in social science from a top Ivy League school. She'd written a book that hadn't sold and started several companies that didn't fulfill her dreams. Kristen had been working successfully in the investment industry. The only problem was the "feast or famine" roller coasters she and her family were on. Things had gotten so bad that, three years prior to her developing a sense of purpose, she and her husband had closed out their retirement account to get by.

As Kristen developed her sense of purpose, which included serving her clients fully, she developed a renewed interest in her

---

* AMP—Think of a time when your creativity was at its highest. What was your sense of purpose and mission at the time?

clients and what she could do for them. She saw their needs in new ways and realized she'd been given considerable resources that she only now wanted to bring into the service of her clients. She began lecturing and training clients in insurance and financial management. She developed tracking programs for their holdings and assessment systems for their needs. She became a veritable fountain of creative ideas in the service of her purpose. Sales came more easily as her clients experienced her seminars and products and the genuine interest she showed in them. As of this writing, she certainly has business cycles—but today's lows are equal to or better than her historic highs.

Purpose drew out creativity by pulling more from Kristen. It engaged her heart and whole being. She saw from a higher perspective when faced with problems, so she came up with bigger and better solutions for her clients.

CORPORATE CREATIVITY

Derek's courage in facing a company crisis, and living true to his higher purpose provides an excellent, inspiring example of corporate-level creativity. Derek's manufacturing concern, which makes processing equipment for the plastics field, employs twenty-five to seventy-five people, depending on the order stream. Derek's father had begun the company, and under him, profits were the company's primary reason for being. Excellent engineering followed. Employees' concerns were not considered. The work force was cut quickly when orders were down, and the interchangeability of all was made clear to each and every one.

Derek became head of the business and ran it for the family. He felt that the company purpose should include the well-being of customers and employees as well as the family. He developed a company purpose statement with his staff and established operating principles to fulfill their purpose. They saw their purpose as serving clients with the highest-quality engineering, manufacturing, and maintenance so they and their clients could live their lives in uplifting ways, experiencing financial, familial, and personal security. The principles of purpose they followed included service, commitment, responsibility, and accountability.

When the company next saw a drop in the order stream, instead of cutting the workforce, Derek brought the employees together, and they came up with ways to increase sales and cut costs. The resulting product innovations were sold as add-ons, new products were introduced in response to client needs, and sales increased. Fewer employees were cut in down times. The company began a new growth curve based on the creativity of a group unified by a compelling higher purpose. Creativity in the service of client needs caused so many innovations in products and services that the company began expanding significantly.

Purpose universally creates the "need" behind the "necessity" which is the mother of invention . . . and more. It's as if we were standing on the summit looking into the valley. We see clearly where we are going, so that when we descend into the valley, we are better oriented. Furthermore, purpose gives us an "elevator" to the summit when we need to see the overview again.

Jack Stack, author of *The Great Game of Business*, heads up an employee-owned company whose purpose includes employee/owner security. Before going onto the shop floor, every employee learns not only what the company is about, but even how to read a balance sheet. This is one of the ways the company ensures a broader perspective, a deeper understanding of the "why" in employees. With a deeper understanding of the "why," employees can more meaningfully fulfill the purpose of the company rather than simply filling limited roles. Each employee looks at things from a broader point of view and contributes at a much higher rate than could be expected without this perspective. Innovations abound and problems are quickly addressed and solved.

CHANGE FROM THE MIDDLE

Miranda is a woman clear of purpose. Her purpose related little to any one aspect of business. She saw her purpose as serving

God wherever she was. Miranda's gift was to bring order to all she did. The day I met Miranda, a room full of volunteers was trying to put together a mass mailing to over 15,000 people around the world. Pandemonium reigned, and little progress was being made. Miranda quietly began walking around the room and talking to people. Within thirty minutes, a tightly co-ordinated production effort was underway.

Miranda is one of the very few people I've met in business who has consistently had the courage to finish jobs and hand them off. She resists the urge to make busywork to justify her ex-istence. Miranda's clarity on higher purpose translates into sys-tems, causing order to develop around her like crystals precipitating out of solution. Most of Miranda's career was spent with a large worldwide information management firm. Miranda had been a saleswoman, district and regional sales manager before moving into the marketing department at the corporate and U.S. operations center.

The company had decentralized in the late '70s, thinking this was a way to be more responsive to the diverse populations it served internationally. Miranda took exception to this. She felt that with changes in technology and business practices around the world, the company needed its resources more focused, co-ordinated, and centralized. She had a plan of her own to make it more competitive into the '90s and bring it back to a more cen-tralized management scheme within five years—a most remark-able feat for a middle manager three levels below the president in one division of a worldwide corporation.

Miranda's plan had power because it furthered the corpo-rate purpose and added to the strength of each division. The core idea in her plan was to develop a unifying sales and ser-vice program that would force technological innovation and unification of the various divisions. She developed a new con-cept of marketing and sales that turned the sales people into highly skilled consultants five to ten years before this type of sales came into vogue. It required a significant improvement in each person's skill set. Several other features of the plan would lead to changes in information storage, warehousing, and product delivery. This represented a major policy and operations shift—not the kind of plan one easily moves through a large international corporation.

At first, Miranda's plan was soundly rejected. Sales had a history of conflict with marketing, and she was caught squarely in the middle. However, her background as a saleswoman and regional sales manager gave her not only information and insight but contacts she could use to further her purposes. She used the Bre'r Rabbit ploy to further her scheme. Just as Bre'r Rabbit begged not to be thrown into the briar patch, from which he could escape, Miranda insisted that the only place for her project to be properly managed and piloted was from marketing, not sales. This offended the national sales group, who fought for the right to "own" the project.

Miranda quite willingly lost this battle but negotiated the right to train the sales force in the new consulting skills. Her project was a resounding success around which the company focused its development plans. Once the training had been completed, Miranda had no work left, so she went to the president and asked if she should take early retirement or a new assignment.

Miranda knew that management information services was a mess. Besides, the next step of her unification plan required moves in this area. She was put in charge of MIS as her last assignment before retiring. With her marketing plan in full force demanding unification, the next compelling force for unification needed to be unleashed, and the heart of information services was just the right place to do it. Miranda felt that the decentralization at a time of extreme technological advance had been an error that could be seen clearly in MIS. In the late '70s and early '80s, corporations had not figured out how to use their computer power fully. For many of them, confused MIS departments were the rule of the day, with high potential and minimal realization.

From her position at the helm of MIS, Miranda was able to bring the divisions together to consider their MIS needs and strategize the department's development. Once again, she was able to marshal key forces to move in the direction of unity.

Within three years of the start of her marketing project, the unification movement in her company was strong. Within five years, it was complete. She retired to serve in her church and pursue her hobby, art.

We could view this as brilliant corporate strategy, but this would miss the point. It does not have the power plays, intrigue, and bad guys usually seen in such moves. Miranda desired no gain in position; she wanted only what she felt was best for the company. To serve and bring order to the world around her was her purpose, and it fit the company need. Her responsibility caused her to avoid petty struggles and keep on course. She allowed no blame and no enemies—only unified purpose and direction. This was not accomplished by control but by intention in expression and total focus on higher purpose. Miranda had virtually no enemies, because she allowed no room for blame or the other accouterments of conflict and victimhood to manifest in her work environment. She exemplified responsibility in action.

Life purpose is an inherent aspect of each one of us. We all create our lives by the moment-to-moment choices we make. Higher purpose guides us to be our best. Its joy, flow, and fulfillment are available at all times. We've seen how John and others discovered the benefits of purpose. Before moving on to developing personal and corporate purpose statements, we will examine others' purpose, how purpose is discovered, just what the common elements of purpose are and how to live the benefits of a purposeful life ourselves.

Chapter 3

Discovering Purpose

In the great scheme of things, what matters is not how long you live, but why you live, what you stand for, and are willing to die for.

...PAUL WATSON, CAPTAIN, THE SEA SHEPHERD SOCIETY

Each of us has an all-encompassing life purpose. In this chapter, we present different ways that people discover, engage in, and conceptualize their life purpose. Some people's sense of mission emerges over their lives. Others discover their purpose through employment, illness, or trauma. A few seem to be born with a clear sense of purpose, while some first identify it in a seminar or with coaching.

Although life purpose can be identified and articulated, it becomes a reality only through living. Many confuse a life purpose statement with life purpose. The statement is no more the purpose than the word Illinois is the state. Just as the word "Illinois" indicates the state and gives us a point of reference, a personal life purpose statement can help us orient to our ultimate aims in our daily life.

The Jigsaw Puzzle

Putting a jigsaw puzzle together without the picture that came on the box is quite challenging. There is a point when we finally realize what the picture is, and the job becomes easier and moves more quickly. Living life is, for most of us, like assembling the jigsaw puzzle without the picture. A clear sense of purpose gives us a better idea of the picture, and then we can lead our lives more powerfully and effectively. Stan experienced this recognition that added power and vision to his life through purpose.

Stan is an economist. For much of his career, he moved from one big deal to another. Some were enormously successful, and others less so. He worked in venture capital, even putting together an expedition that recovered the largest sunken treasure ever discovered before 1981. However, he had no higher sense of purpose to guide him. Money was his highest aim. He wanted wealth to secure him against life's disappointments. His life moves were bold but erratic. He represented a significant resource with little meaning or direct contribution to the general good of the world around him.

He then discovered his life purpose, which he further clarified in a purpose seminar: to help people live better lives by appreciating the value of life. He fought tough battles and grew stronger in purpose. He began settling down, learning to enjoy what he was doing. He no longer looked for the big hit to make him happy, because his life was more fulfilled each day.

Stan's Story

> *Happiness is to take up the struggle in the midst of the raging storm and not to pluck the lute in the moonlight or recite poetry among the blossoms.*
>
> ...DING LING, *THE SUN*

Stan was working at a world-renowned economic consulting firm when his life purpose came into focus. A creative young Chicago attorney asked him to assess the economic impact of a wrongful death on the ultimate earnings of an auto-repair garage owner.

The story was this: An older teen had walked into a knitting shop and grabbed the cash in the register. The owner, emerging from the back room, saw him run out the door. Recognizing the thief, the owner ran, yelling at him until he dropped the money. The police were notified, and a bulletin went out over the police radio.

To the thief's dismay, his battery was so run down that his car wouldn't start. He ran to an auto-repair garage, co-owned by a father and son, where he was known. The mechanic-son, not knowing about the theft, told the thief to get into his own car, and they drove toward the thief's car to give him a jump start.

An off-duty policeman had heard the police transmission and donned his uniform to begin patrolling for the thief. He saw the mechanic and pulled the car over. Holding his revolver at the driver's head, he yelled three times, "Hands up, [expletive]!" The driver, bewildered and unaware of the situation, hesitated and reached for his wallet. At this movement, the police officer shot him through the temple, killing him instantly.

The story became common knowledge, and the mechanic's already bereaved parents were even more upset that the death certificate improperly identified their son with the theft. The sheriff and police repeatedly refused their request to have it corrected, so they went to an attorney for help.

At this point, their only concern was to set the record straight. The attorney felt out of his depth and contacted a Chicago law firm. Seemingly unimportant to the firm, the case sat collecting dust until Doug Rallo, the young Chicago attorney, came across it. His drive and creativity brought into question both the loss of the mechanic's business that he ran with his father and a revolutionary concept; the loss of the value of life he had suffered in this wrongful death. Until this point, only lost income had been used to value a lost life.

Stan was moved by how helpless the parents were against the bureaucracy and how innocent was their pursuit of a clean record for their son. He was also acutely aware of how little direction the jury would have in arriving at a proper award. Until this time, American law recognized loss of income as the only value of life. Monetary awards, called punitive damages, could also be assessed to punish wrongdoers. This approach left the impression that the CEO of a large company had lost more than those in lower positions, because his potential earnings were greater.

Correcting this inequity, Stan drew instead on the substantial academic body of knowledge in economics wherein life is valued by what we spend to save it. He helped the jury arrive at an award reflecting the actual loss of life, the loss of the pleasure of life, or hedonic damages.

This and subsequent actions have been called the most significant introductions into tort law, or the law of liability, in the 1980s. Economists and lawyers are polarized on this issue and have been fighting about it since. Stan's life has been threatened, and books and courses have been developed in vain to show attorneys how to beat him in court. He stands up bravely to these assaults, because he has found a purpose for his life—to help us all appreciate and value the life we have. He's never forgotten the plight of that Joliet family or the thousands of others whom he serves. His talents of analysis and persuasion and his interest in the well-being of others come together in this mission.

His quest to learn to value life and help us learn extends to his home life, too. In a seminar on "purpose," he saw for the first time how his work and personal missions come together in his life purpose. Every aspect of his life is defined by this quest. He "sees" the pattern in the puzzle—what he plans with his family and what he does elsewhere all fit. He is learning to value his life in all its manifestations. His actions are determined by their impact on his purpose as he understands and discovers it. His time with himself, his children, and friends is all part of his purpose—he lives his life to contribute and be contributed to, to love fully and be loved, since loves seems, to him, the ultimate asset or source of life.

Not all people experience the certainty of Stan once they discover their purpose. For them, their clarity of vision and purpose develop over time, with effort and hesitation. The change to living a purposeful life is often gradual and requires the development of many new life and business skills.

DEVELOPING PURPOSEFUL BUSINESS OVER TIME: AN EVOLUTIONARY JOURNEY

Marsha

> *You will become as small as your controlling desire; great as your dominant aspiration.*
>
> ...JAMES ALLEN, COMMITMENT TO EXCELLENCE

Marsha is a stockbroker. She started in the early 1980s, when people were making a significant profit just about anywhere they put their money. She prided herself on good stock tips, and her company was rarely wrong. Marsha was really shaken in 1987 when she lost two-thirds of her personal capital because she had overleveraged herself in futures. Many of her clients were similarly hurt. The shock of her fallibility carried through all her subsequent business. Her confidence shaken, she feared calling many of her regular clients. She began relying on mailings instead, routinely making up to one hundred twenty follow-up calls per day in her search of investors! For her, the game was numbers and information that gave her clients an edge. She thought her only value to clients was to come up with a good product or tip, and these were never certain, so her client relations felt forever tenuous.

Although she was superficially charming, in fact she calculated a person's net worth quickly and moved on immediately if he or she did not qualify. People had become objects to her, and new products or stock tips were her bait to attract these objects. By 1994, Marsha had come close to her pre-1987 income only once. Her highest purpose was to make money, and her life was relatively joyless.

In 1994, she joined a sales support group I led. She wanted help finding more customers. The group's focus on higher purpose and service almost caused her to quit at first. She found it excruciating to identify a higher purpose, since the highest she had looked was the best yield, the most undervalued stock, and, ultimately, the next sale.

Higher purpose to her was a distraction from sales. "Service" was to her a platitudinous advertising ploy to lure investors. Marsha found it terrifying simply to relax and converse with potential clients. If they didn't qualify with a high enough net worth, she felt compelled to move on, for fear of missing the next sale. Enjoyment for her was limited to the fleeting relief of big commissions; the rest was agony.

Over time, Marsha learned to relax and converse with potential clients in more depth. Her clients began disclosing more, and, to her surprise, she began selling more diverse products. One person she almost discounted eventually disclosed a seventy-five-thousand-dollar savings account for her children's college tuition. Marsha helped her move this to a secure higher-performing vehicle and didn't make anything on the transaction. Instead, she experienced real fulfillment—and ultimately received several referrals to boot.

Marsha's alignment with higher purpose has been gradual. She has begun seeing herself as an educator, advisor, and co-voyager with her clients. No longer does she live so much in terror of an investor unhappy because a sure winner she had proposed went sour. Less and less does she hungrily eye people as meat to be consumed. She is leaving behind her frantic approach to the phone. She still cranks out the numbers but relaxes into conversation and delights in the wide variety of ways her clients relate to their money.

She has begun seeing herself as a life-purpose advisor—helping clients achieve their desires and ultimately, financial security. Lives that she previously used are now blessings with which she is gifted. She has developed new standards of behavior. Integrity now means telling the whole truth, service means supporting the whole person, and caring means genuine heart-to-heart contact.

For some time, Marsha straddled two boats that were drifting further apart. Her old habit of selling at all costs persisted until she could make the leap of working from higher purpose. She needed to learn new skills as she developed into a genuine investment advisor, teaching classes and leading investment support groups. These new skills, however, have helped her further fulfill her higher purpose, which she sees as developing the skills of financial mastery and service to enhance her own security and that of her clients. She enjoys being a co-voyager, no longer the flimflam answer woman. More and more people refer their friends to her. As she grows in skill and compassion, she prospers financially.

Marsha is continually developing new skills to complete her transition. She is becoming a better listener, problem solver, and coach. Her facility with financial tools is increasing, and she is even finding more challenge and fulfillment in her marriage as she becomes a better communicator. Marsha feels a deeper sense of relaxation because she is beginning to listen to her deepest yearnings. Her natural sense of integrity and desire to serve are beginning to receive full attention under the light of her expanding sense of purpose. For her, a sense of purpose is an evolving affair, a journey she is taking, and a battle to be fought daily as she seeks to replace frantic, hungry searching with deep, meaningful contact one day at a time. **(AMP)***

EVOLVING PURPOSE, DEVELOPING GIFTS

> *Believe that you have the destiny, the innate ability, to become all you expect of life. Experience all of life's peaks and plateaus. Find the meaning of life's struggles and accomplishments. There you will find the meaning to life and life's work.*
>
> …Sherrie Householder, Creeds to Live By, Dreams to Follow, ed. S.P. Schultz

We met Ellis in Chapter 2. Ellis graduated from Harvard with a Ph.D. in sociology. We saw how his pre-purpose goals were to be

---

* AMP—Think of someone who seems driven by lower purpose. What is the difference between this person's attitude and life and the attitude of those who seem to orient to higher purpose? What do you think he or she will need to shift like Marsha?

famous and rich. Teachers and other adults had acknowledged his brain power ever since he could remember, and he was sure his brains would win him the fame and riches he coveted.

Ellis's book—that he was sure would be a best-seller—didn't even sell out the first printing. He opened a chain of bookstores, only to sell them to cover his debts. Finally, Ellis found his way into consulting, buying the rights to a corporate training program. At first, he was excited by the money he could make selling and delivering this program.

He moved his wife and children into a very expensive house but soon hit the skids. Ellis found the work boring, and his sales activity was erratic. He would sell when he needed money but languish between times. He hated his job and began yearning for a way out. Despite the enormous profit potential, Ellis was so erratic that he had to sell his house to get through an especially long sales drought.

He planned over and over to work hard and produce at full potential for five years and then retire, but these plans always broke down. He couldn't string two strong years together, let alone five. He repeatedly failed to maintain his enthusiasm—until he began taking seminars on quality of life. In these sessions, he discovered the reasons behind his original goals of fame and riches.

Ellis learned that he wanted money to make up for his lack of enjoyment in everyday life, and he wanted fame to fill the deep hole he felt inside from feeling worthless. He tracked this back to being told as a child by his mother that he was unlovable. He began to develop compassion for himself. This understanding led him into the full possibilities of his career. As his work became more personal, he began relating to his clients more as people rather than as stepping-stones. He learned to enjoy them more and got to know them better, which led him to care about them more deeply.

This caring caused him to want his clients to have the same quality of life and enjoyment he had discovered. He began engaging in deeper and more extensive levels of service to his clients. His single product became the hub for a wheel of products

Ellis developed to meet his clients' needs. His ability to contribute to his clients excited him, and his Ivy League social science background allowed him to develop tools of the highest quality.

Ellis had discovered his life purpose: to use his full capacities to enjoy life and succeed so that he could help his clients enjoy life and succeed. His reputation spread, and today he has the money and renown he always wanted. Most of all, however, he has a sense of fulfillment that comes from making full use of his talents and living a purposeful life.

The nature of Ellis's work evolved from product sales to deep personal service. He learned to develop his gifts in direct response to the needs of his clients. As he did this, his sense of purpose clarified and became a powerful beacon by which he could guide his company and the rest of his life. Ellis himself became an example to many others, who began to find their own sense of mission as they worked for him or received coaching from him.

Each of us can live our higher purpose more fully by taking stock and adjusting course, as Ellis did. We all have unreasonable, irrelevant, or almost magical solutions for our happiness—like his goals of fame and money. If we look behind these "solutions" to identify our deepest yearnings, we will find our deepest selves, the seeds of our ultimate life purpose. **(AMP)***

EVOLUTION AND CRISIS

Jack Stack is president of Springfield Remanufacturing Company, an employee-owned engine remanufacturer, and author of *The Great Game of Business*. His evolving sense of purpose was brought to focus in a crisis, one that threatened a summary layoff of the entire work force he headed.

---

* AMP 1—Think of people who seem to be operating from the wrong motivation. What do you think they would need to make the adjustment that Ellis made?

* AMP 2—Think of something you did for the "wrong" reasons. How did it turn out? What did you learn? What would you do differently?

He begins his story by explaining why he was classified 4F and unable to go to Vietnam. The draft meant a lack of higher-quality young managers in the major worldwide heavy equipment manufacturer for which he worked. This lack created a vacuum that sucked him rapidly through numerous positions in the company, from warehousing to purchasing to manufacturing to personnel, eleven positions in eleven years.

In one memorable sequence, production was at a standstill while one of his team members told him they couldn't get new parts without going through the impossible checking and ordering procedure established by "some [expletive] in purchasing."

That "[expletive]" was Jack himself, in one of his previous jobs. Seeing the results of uninformed, uncoordinated, decision making from many perspectives gave him a healthy respect for the importance of communication, coordination, alignment, and integration throughout businesses. He developed into a leader of champion production units and was sent far and wide throughout the company to turn around underperforming operations.

He had just succeeded in turning around the engine reproduction plant in Springfield when he heard rumors that the company intended to close it. Outraged and concerned for the employees affected, he and several others mortgaged their houses (a courageous move in the face of unemployment) and bought the unit. They endured big debt and hard times but have consistently grown and been growing strongly for years.

Today, they are an employee-owned and -operated firm that practices what they call "open-book" management. This approach requires full disclosure of numbers and follows the principles of inclusion, alignment, communication, and other principles of purpose, even though they don't necessarily identify them as such. Jack writes and speaks widely in his mission to make business rational and inclusive.

Jack's purpose—to enhance personal security for employees through education and ownership—evolved and was brought to clear focus in the face of a crisis. If each of us does our job in the best way possible, learns our lessons, we, too, will evolve a sense of purpose. We may or may not have a crisis to bring it all to focus, and we probably won't be writing and speaking like Jack, but we will be working and influencing those around us, playing our part in the evolution of mankind. **(AMP)***

LIFE CIRCUMSTANCES

You see things and say 'why?', but I dream things that never were and I say 'why not?'

...GEORGE BERNARD SHAW

Circumstances often compel us to manifest our life purpose. One of the most famous examples of this dynamic is Mohandas K. (Mahatma) Gandhi. Gandhi, an Indian, was admitted to the bar in England after a traditional British education. He had occasion to travel to South Africa to represent a case. His first experience of racism, South African style, came when he was thrown off the train for refusing to move from his properly ticketed first-class seat to a substandard section for "coloreds"—any non-whites, including blacks, Asians, and Indians. Outraged at this treatment, he went to prominent members of the South African "colored" community to complain. To his dismay, they all regularly submitted to the indignities of South African racism without a fight. Their financial security depended on compliance.

"Coloreds" were required by law to carry identity cards. This offended his sense of propriety and seemed like the proper place to begin his protest. He mobilized several key members of the non-European, nonwhite community to join him in a demonstration to burn their identity cards. He was beaten and thrown into jail. Gandhi then began a number of legal and public-relations battles he was to win over the South African government because of his mastery of the law and his dedication to what was right. International newspaper coverage was sympathetic to his cause, spotlighting South African brutality.

---

* AMP—Describe a life crisis or trauma that helped you or someone you know develop a clearer sense of meaning or life purpose—a clearer sense of what was really important in your/their life.

International volunteers and financial support flowed into South Africa, requiring that Gandhi establish an "ashram," or spiritual community. Gandhi waged his battle on spiritual principles acceptable to the Jews, Hindus, and Christians who flocked around him. The movement was committed to nonviolence, fearlessly standing for basic human rights with love and compassion. It was his firm belief that cruelty was ended with kindness—not more cruelty, violence, or force. Gandhi's ashram grew into a movement and he won most of the concessions for which he struggled, returning to India a hero.

Once in India, Gandhi eschewed a life of certain political success, choosing instead to live the life of a peasant. He explored the problems of a divided, colonized India firsthand and then published his findings, providing a focal point for both the liberation and unification of British-ruled India. On at least one occasion, he fasted to near death in protest of injustice or violence in the political process. Gandhi lived true to his principles: nonviolence, choice, love, compassion, and consciousness. He impeccably applied these principles even when the power to control and dominate was in his hands. Under Gandhi's guidance, India obtained freedom from Great Britain, Nehru was made unified India's first elected leader, and the healing of years of division and dominance began.

Gandhi's life represents a life purpose brought to focus by circumstances. The same can happen to each of us in our daily lives. Following his example, we can stand up for what we believe, live true to higher principles, and follow our hearts. He envisioned a free, effective India. There is no reason each of us cannot realize our own vision of a better life. **(AMP)***

---

* AMP—Remember a time you failed to take a stand for what you believed. What was the effect on you? Do you remember a time when you wanted to or did act to address some wrong you perceived in a situation? What stand did you take (or want to take)? What principles or values were you upholding?

Visionaries With Purpose

The air travel industry began when the Wright brothers envisioned the freedom of powered flight. We've all heard of Fulton's folly, the development of the auto, the telephone, the electric light, and many similar cases of people following their dreams. These dreamers are the leaders of humanity—people like Joan of Arc, Washington, Jefferson, Rosa Parks, Franklin, Schweitzer, Curie, Mandela, Anthony, King, Gandhi, Tubman, and more.

New company policies and innovations are made daily because an employee makes a stand for what is right and keeps on standing until others join in and the organization changes. We saw in Chapter 2 how Miranda caused a major worldwide corporation to reorganize and prosper because of the strength of her conviction.

Gandhi's impeccable adherence to higher principles caused two nations, India and South Africa, to go through major changes. He and Miranda did this by staying true to their higher principles: with them they were able to navigate foggy terrain with unerring steps.

In Chapters 7 and 10, on personal and corporate principles, we will see how to apply the principles of purpose to enhance personal power and guide us through uncertainties in our daily life to our greatest contributions.

CASEY

Be what you are, and become what you are capable of becoming.
...ROBERT LOUIS STEVENSON, *CREEDS TO LIVE BY,*
DREAMS TO FOLLOW, ED. S.P. SCHULTZ

Casey didn't come from the best of homes. His parents neglected and abused him as a child. In his words, he wasn't gifted "with the greatest computer" between his ears, and he barely made it through high school. He wonders what would have become of him if it hadn't been for his baseball coaches taking an interest in him. He figures he was good in baseball because he always stayed vigilant in the field, a vigilance learned at home to avoid his father's drunken rages.

Vigilance was a skill that got Casey promoted to warehouse manager at several places he worked. Vigilance got him fired when he treated the plant managers like the enemy. It wasn't until his third firing that Casey faced the problem and changed. He saw the unconscious pain from his childhood that was driving him and he discovered the positive intent to his problem: to protect him. Unfortunately, this more than protected him in business, because he got hurt instead. He wanted the management and office staff to like him, but he'd just bite their heads off at the slightest hint of problems. They were afraid of him, and he was afraid of them.

Some coaching, a good deal of soul-searching, and joining a men's group gave Casey the support he needed to shift. He kept the sense of vigilance operating to ensure excellence in "his" warehouse but shifted it from distrust of coworkers to concern for the company well-being. Today, Casey sees himself as responsible for the success of the front office, manufacturing, and the entire company. He figures that in some way, all aspects of the operation depend on his warehouse. He has shifted his personal purpose from one of protection to one of teamwork and success.

Instead of glowering at the plant manager, he has developed a good-natured, joking relationship that even extends to the president on his visits to Casey's operation. He takes pride in the company, and the company takes pride in him. His sense of purpose has become an inspiration to his employees in the warehouse and on the loading dock, as well as others he sees daily.

Casey's last firing led him to discover a misplaced sense of purpose. Many of us have a misplaced sense of purpose like Casey. We call these reactive purposes. Casey gives us an inspiring example of transforming reactive purpose into creative purpose. Just as he transformed from protection to contribution, we can all use higher purpose to raise our level of personal performance and participation.

FINDING (LEARNING) PURPOSE THROUGH TRAUMA

The things which hurt instruct.
...BENJAMIN FRANKLIN

Sally was the third of four children. Her father was killed in a hunting accident when she was eight years old. As the oldest girl, she was made responsible for the baby, food preparation, and the house while her mother returned to work.

In grade school, one of her teachers told her mother that Sally would never be an A student. Sally got A's from then on through hard work and determination. She wanted to go to college and be a nurse, but her mother wouldn't hear of it, saying that hairdressers made good money. Sally did neither, getting married and going to work in the oil industry.

Sally was a battered wife, suffering five broken ribs and a cracked vertebra after one particularly horrendous beating. She suffered from severe arthritis by the time she was in her mid-thirties and was told that she needed another back operation; indeed, there were days when she couldn't get out of bed. During and after her marriage, she had thirteen surgeries and almost died four times. She developed leukemia and was expecting to die young when a series of events changed the course of her life.

In the mid-'80s Sally remarried. At the same time, her cherished boss at the oil company quit. With the encouragement of her new, loving husband, she also quit shortly thereafter to heal herself. Fearing for her life, she saw a homeopathic physician, who taught her meditation. Within three months her spine had healed without surgery, and her leukemia no longer showed in tests. Her body was free from pain for the first time in her memory.

She had discovered what she wanted to do with her life—help others who suffered as she had. She studied hard and is, years later, an established healer, still pain free and with no sign of leukemia. Sally regards her earlier life as having prepared her for her ultimate purpose, which she today sees as assisting the planet and its inhabitants in the healing process. She can't imagine how she could fulfill this purpose without her earlier traumas. She says she wouldn't trade the earlier pain for anything—without it, she couldn't fully appreciate the pain of others or wouldn't have had the necessary motivation to follow her pioneering path. Once again we see purpose evolving from wounding or earlier trauma.

Ultimately, our sense of purpose evolves out of our being who we are at our core, our essence. Purpose is heavily influenced by our gifts and personal history. It is a natural capacity we all have that flows from living life true to our highest vision, developing our capacities as fully as did Ellis in our first story and taking care of our personal unfinished businesses, as did Casey and Sally. Purpose flows when we satisfy our yearnings, from basic to sublime.

In every one of us is a pragmatic Jack Stack, a creative Ellis, and a saintly Gandhi. For some of us, purpose is living God's greatest plan, while for others it is living true to our highest self. Regardless of how we conceptualize it, purpose means living the most fulfilling, meaningful life possible.

A life of purpose and power is part of our essence. As we saw in Casey's example, not all of us manifest great worldly power or wield wide public influence. For many of us, a clear sense of purpose provides the power to generate and serve that we saw in Ellis. Purpose helps us be more creative, lovingly support a family and help them be their best, steadfastly stand by friends in success and in need. Clear, purposeful interaction transforms every human endeavor and interaction.

It's almost as if we are part of an army of life—a war is being fought within each of us for our highest selves. The battleground is our every thought, deed, and action. Our position in the hierarchy is irrelevant, since the ultimate success of humanity depends on all of us being good soldiers and playing our part. Consider the body as a whole, imagine that each part wants to be the best it can be to add to the whole. What a mess we would be in if the knee wanted to be the heart! Fulfilling its own purpose is necessary and sufficient for each part and the body's ultimate success. If only each of us could be equally clear and focused as our body parts.

Before developing our own purpose statements, we will examine the elements common to purpose. This examination will give us a stronger vision and sense of what we are doing when we move on to purpose statement development.

Chapter 4

The Essence of Purpose, What it Does for You

Life is either a daring adventure or it is nothing at all.
...HELEN KELLER

Babies and little children live with a natural sense of purpose. Just watch their intensity and concentration as they play with a mobile over the crib or examine their feet. What a marvel to watch a toddler charge from one object of interest to another. There is a purposeful intensity to all they do—sleeping, playing, laughing, or crying. At this stage of their lives, they are intensely and purposefully exploring the world, learning about physical reality, and developing their capacity to influence and be influenced by the world around them. For a child, enthusiastically throwing food from the high chair (with the required squeals of delight) is purposeful activity. At such times, children are developing mastery of their physical universe and giving their lungs a good workout at the same time.

Deeply personal, purposeful behavior begins to dim in us as children as we become socialized. By the time we are adults, we have developed unconscious fears and comfortable limiting habits that make fully purposeful living more difficult to realize, thus we unconsciously give up our birthright.

Most of us must develop a purposeful lifestyle, just as we develop any skill. We do this by articulating our purpose, living by it to the best of our ability, identifying the principles of purpose, and keeping our activities attuned to them. We do it by becoming excited about our purpose and the goals that go along with it. We experience an urgency that causes us to learn to use our resources more efficiently. This urgency pulls us forward into lives of fulfillment. We live more life in less time.

We learn to move quickly between challenges the way young children race between points of interest. We move quickly because purpose draws us urgently forward. We revel in our capacity to do things, just as children enjoy the excitement of running. As adults, we must make it a point to maintain this sense of vitality. Young children engage in it without thinking, but many of us need the conscious discipline of living "on purpose"—a routine just like exercising to keep in shape. A clear sense of purpose helps motivate us to be our best. We must engage in purposeful activity to develop our natural capacity for living an engaged life. As we identify the common elements of purpose, we deepen our appreciation of the breadth and power of purposeful living. In fact, living the elements of purpose alone would automatically lead to the benefits of having a clear life purpose, including the ability to ultimately articulate what we are about.

Life purpose is not some "airy-fairy," far-out rarity. It is a capacity and task of all humans. Purposeful living is our natural state, one we must reclaim. In becoming socialized, we've all been conditioned to live "off purpose." Most of us learn to live first by society's norms before we learn to live true to our own deepest yearnings. It is our job to apply ourselves fully to uncovering these deepest yearnings and living purposefully.

A NATURAL CAPACITY UNCOVERED

The word education comes from the Latin educare, to draw out. We can only learn and develop what we already are; our deepest, most essential selves.

Francesca was born with an abundance of talents. As a child, she exuded energy as she dove into life. She was brilliant, an excellent athlete, and extremely attractive. But her father committed suicide when Francesca was a child, and her already protective mother severely limited Francesca's activities out of a fear of losing her too.

Francesca did well in school and was popular, but always held back. Her natural sense of purpose was severely inhibited. Even though she showed promise, she never came through to meet her or others' expectations. She became a professional public-relations specialist and fund-raiser for several community organizations, moving from job to job hoping to find "the right one." She always felt like a marginal member wherever she worked. She was fully engaged only in sports, where she was an especially fierce competitor.

Finally, she found work as a planner and fund-raiser for an agency in which she really believed. Things still did not improve. She was critical of management and was, once again, on the fringe. Her criticisms of management were accurate, but she herself did nothing to change the way the organization functioned. In fact, she was doing so poorly at raising money that the life of the organization was in jeopardy. She realized that her own contribution was no better than that of the management she criticized.

Finally, Francesca decided to get professional coaching to help her perform to her potential. First, she took a hard look at herself, developed herself toward her ideal, and articulated her life purpose—to support the development of a genuine, just society that honored and fully supported all its members. Then she began measuring her daily activity against this. Slowly she caught fire, began initiating projects, pushing herself and others to perform at a higher level and generally operating with a greater sense of purposeful urgency. She began working with the same ferocity she showed in sports. Her whole life began coming into focus as her natural sense of purpose emerged. Creativity seemed to be her middle name as she joined and became a leader in several volunteer organizations.

She was no longer on the periphery—her natural sense of purpose led her to the heart of everything she did. She began developing her talents fully. Her life became an adventure as she ran from one challenge to the next, just as she had done in childhood. Her childhood purposeful behavior had developed into a mature adult purpose, a life dedicated to bringing her creativity and excellence into the development of social justice.

Recognizing the elements common to lives of purpose, we can begin to unlock this natural capacity in ourselves. We saw this natural capacity explode in Stan as he moved from being a deal maker to a life enhancer. Marsha unlocked her natural urge to serve, overcame her feelings of scarcity, and began serving her clients better. Ellis reoriented his life to focus on service, and Casey became an integral corporate team member. All the examples we have reviewed so far show us people releasing their potential, their native capacities coming to the foreground as they begin to apply their whole beings to ultimate purpose. **(AMP)***

INTEGRITY

It's treating each other right, and having the courage to say you are wrong when you are wrong. That's all part of business, and it's part of the big picture.

...JACK STACK

When she uncovered her innate purpose, Francesca's life began fitting better. She was more at the center of things and the diverse parts of her life had a common sense and meaning. They fitted together like the sounds from different instruments blending to create a beautiful tune. She was more honest and depend-

---

* AMP—Think of a situation where you expressed or developed a talent or capacity through full immersion in an activity. What was it like being fully engaged? How did it feel to experience full expression of a talent or skill level?

able at work, and this led to a greater sense of satisfaction for her. She was living and working with more wholeness and integrity.

When we do work we don't respect, when we strongly disagree but say nothing, when money dictates our activity to the exclusion of our hearts, we compromise our integrity. Compromising our integrity, we cannot feel whole and complete. Without integrity, a sense of purpose is much more difficult to maintain. We lose the power that comes from synergy—all the parts of our lives fitting together.

Higher purpose is always accompanied by greater integrity or wholeness. Purpose is an expression of our deepest, most essential, integral selves. It not only engages our entire being but draws out our most essential nature. We become more whole, and our lives feel more complete. We live with greater belongingness, genuineness, and power.

Integrity means wholeness. A body with integrity has all its parts. When we speak of the integrity of a ship's hull, we mean that the hull is whole and complete. Living a purposeful life leads to an increasing sense of wholeness and personal substance. We take the difficult stands like Gandhi and become more powerful, generating, and dependable, like Casey and Marsha.

Hannah

Integrity enhances purpose and purpose fosters integrity. Hannah discovered this in both her daily activity at work and the larger aspects of her career.

Hannah graduated near the top of her class from one of the world's top schools of finance. She was snapped up by a leading financial institution with a major venture capital division. Her strategy was to begin in banking finance and work her way into her desired specialty, venture capital. She could have gone directly into less prestigious venture firms but decided she was better off in the well-known, more respected institution, even though the job wasn't what she wanted.

Eight years later, Hannah was still in banking, as a small player servicing major accounts. Her career had not moved the way she had imagined. She was sullen and did just enough to get by. She performed well because of her basic skills but was not applying herself, and everyone knew it. She conflicted with almost every man she dealt with. One senior officer seemed to consider it his mission in life to make her look bad and block her career.

Hannah's decision to take a position she hadn't wanted, because of the prestige of the firm and the top salary, had backfired. It lacked integrity for her. She had sold herself to the highest, most prestigious bidder without concern for her own satisfaction and fulfillment. She was circling in a backwater, stagnating and going nowhere fast. The golden handcuffs had been placed on her wrists, and what had seemed a small breach of integrity was now a major rift.

Hannah's original breach of integrity had occurred when she chose prestige, money, and position over substance and her heart's desire. This meant engaging in work that didn't fully interest her, so she failed to engage totally or perform to her potential. This failure of performance, along with her conflicts with key men in the company, led to a frustrating situation perpetuated by the golden handcuff of a top salary in a prestigious firm.

Hannah was unclear about her purpose. Her whole life was becoming a sham, because her heart was not in anything she did. She constantly thought of quitting and becoming a poet or social worker.

Hannah showed uncommon courage when she finally came to grips with her mistake and decided to bite the bullet. She took a middle-level position with a much smaller venture-capital management firm, where she earned a much lower base salary but could anticipate an ultimately much higher income with top performance and a generous bonus plan.

Hannah had taken a major step to restore the integrity in her career and moved significantly toward greater clarity in her career purpose. Her life no longer felt like a lie, and she thought less and less about quitting or dropping out to be a poet or social worker. Her charity work increased, and her creative urges were satisfied by new challenges both at work and in her personal life. Having managed the career move so well, she couldn't have imagined the new challenges to her integrity that awaited her.

The firm she had joined consisted of seven venture "partners." One of them, Elizabeth, was actually a partner in the holding firm from which most of the capital came. Elizabeth was boss, and the others in the "partners group" were actually employees called partners because of their specialties in marketing, sales, finance, operations, or regulations. They also received phantom stock in the operation and were rewarded as owners.

The partners operated as a board of directors for all of their acquisitions. Each partner also had primary responsibility for identification and management of certain acquisitions. The amount of control exercised varied, depending on the company's position in each holding. It could mean an advisory capacity in a minority position or active management in majority to full-ownership positions.

Hannah worked for Elizabeth and all the other partners. She was in charge of finance and deal structuring. She managed relations with both financial and legal institutions for all the partners. She was highly enthused to have her career "on track," as she put it.

Her excitement was dampened when Rob, the marketing genius of the group, began asking her to change numbers for one of his new pet acquisitions. He always had good reasons for his changes, but Hannah became increasingly uncomfortable with the situation.

Hannah was frequently included in the partners' meetings, where she noticed another disturbing trend. Rob rarely followed through on Elizabeth's requests. When Hannah asked him why, she was told things like, "Elizabeth never knows what she really wants or needs."

Over time, the bad faith between Rob and Elizabeth became increasingly uncomfortable for Hannah. She didn't want to be disloyal to Rob, but being loyal to Rob meant being disloyal to Elizabeth. Her mixed emotions boiled until she clarified for herself that her purpose was to serve the company and that her primary loyalties were to the truth and the company's well-being.

She began constantly reviewing her purpose and reminding herself to do unto others as she would have done unto her. She began confronting Rob with problems and supporting Elizabeth in her initiatives. Following her behind-the-scenes confrontations with Rob, she began standing up to him in partners' meetings. Things heated up to the point where Rob wanted her fired, and Elizabeth intervened.

At the time of this writing, Rob is slated to be terminated after the next divestiture, and Hannah is in line for a partner slot. As her sense of purpose clarified, her integrity increased. Her sense of wholeness was enhanced, and her self-respect improved dramatically. She developed more personal substance, worked harder than ever, and took stands she was proud of. Her relationships with men in the company improved, too. As one of the male senior partners noticed her integrity, he began mentoring her and helping in her career development.

Whether we are artists, writers, homemakers, or businessmen, living with purpose compels us to more genuine expression. Through increasing integrity of expression, we experience more wholeness and likelihood of success. We may be fired from one job, but we are more likely to eventually end up in an institution that shares our values and furthers our life purpose. **(AMP)***

---

* AMP 1—How would you rate your current job on a "wholeness scale" from 0-10? (0, very limited use of yourself on the job; 10, full use of all your qualities , talents, and resources.) What's missing in your current job? What could you do that would lead to a fuller expression of your whole self on the job?

* AMP 2—Rate your current job on an integrity scale from 0-10. (0, no integrity, no morality, sleazy operation, bad faith everywhere; 10, high level of ethics and standards, good faith among employees and with customers.) What, if anything, would you like to do to increase the level of integrity in your job or organization? What do you feel stops you from doing this?

LEARNING AND GROWING

When an archer misses the mark, he turns and looks for the fault within himself. Failure to hit the bull's-eye is never the fault of the target. To improve your aim, improve yourself.

...GILBERT ARLAND, COMMITMENT TO EXCELLENCE

Learning, growing, and developing are aspects common to all purpose development. Gandhi learned the law but had to learn to lead before he reached clarity of purpose. He then learned compassion and rational change. Jack Stack learned about the manufacturing business, then learned to run an employee-owned company. Ellis learned how to develop product, supervise, and consult. Sally grew through personal healing, and Casey developed into a team player.

People with a clear sense of purpose consistently learn, grow, and experience. In learning, we know things today that we did not know yesterday. In growing, we develop skills or capacities we lacked. We have seen this in all our previous examples and will see even more. People who consistently learn, grow, and develop are more likely to have a clear sense of purpose. If we continue to face our weaknesses and learn the skills to overcome them, we will advance and be more able to serve when it is demanded of us, and it is more likely to be demanded of us. Following purpose puts us face to face with these lessons.

Learning and growing develops our gifts and calls us to self-realization. Self-realization is an interesting concept, which really means realizing or making a reality of our potential. Possibilities are made actualities through the lessons we learn and ways we develop.

Learning and growing are enhanced when we begin to focus more clearly on a higher purpose. We begin to face barriers we've avoided and develop new skills necessary to get over or around the new barriers we face. Shane exemplifies this phenomenon clearly.

Shane came from pious religious stock—members of his family were among the first settlers of the Northwest. His father was a successful attorney, and his mother had developed one of the most elite corporate accounting firms on the West coast. Wanting to make it on his own, Shane came to Chicago and began his accounting career at the bottom of one of the cities' better-known firms.

He worked his way up to partner and key account manager for the company's largest client. Disdainful of all the wining and dining he was asked to do, he generally looked down his nose at the entire firm, harshly judging the required glad-handing and favor exchanging. He had developed no genuine personal friends in his dealings with coworkers or clients and was just waiting for the day he could leave the "dirty" world of business and devote himself to becoming a minister. Shane suffered from the good/bad dualism we see in many high-minded business people and he blamed his failure to live up to his ideals on his environment.

As it turns out, Shane was made of better stuff. Discussing his feelings with his spiritual advisor, he recognized that his dualistic way of thinking was limiting him. He "caught fire" with a desire to unify his conflicting sides and dove back into his company with a clear sense of mission—to live his religion fully in all aspects of his life, especially work—he dedicated himself specifically to follow the truth and dedicate himself to the company's success and wholeness.

He saw his hypocrisy with his key account and transferred the client to another partner, beginning to develop a whole new area of consulting for the firm. His new venture placed him in increasing contact with the senior partners—a group he had universally reviled—forcing him to fight a number of battles for resources and policy. He began learning a whole new set of management skills. He discovered how much goodwill he had missed because of his black-and-white judgment. He had to develop subordinates and champion his new department.

At first he clung to his views that the senior partners and their "flunkies" were still the corrupt group he perceived. He dove into battle zealously, only to discover more and more that they were much more decent than he had imagined. They were trying to communicate with him and work things out. They had been all along. He had projected a great deal of unwarranted negativity onto them. He wondered how many friendly gestures he had missed.

His coworkers rose in Shane's esteem, and his skills in corporate maneuvering developed rapidly. His venture was a grand success. Anticipated revenues tripled in his first year of operations. This could have been his ticket out of the firm, giving him the chance to make a killing on his own and then devote himself full-time to his "real" ministry. But it was not to be. Shane had learned and grown from his sense of mission and could no longer claim to be the only one in a white hat.

He'd seen his own dark side and realized that much of the darkness he saw in others was a projection of his own hidden aspects. He was growing both personally and professionally. His business ministry, as he called his professional mission, began to take shape in a worklife of truth, strength, and compassion. And his professional skills were growing at a most gratifying rate. He had learned that the "good guy/bad guy" world of his fantasies did not exist and that there was good in everyone and darkness in everyone, including himself. This learning led to a virtual explosion of growth in his development of the new venture.

Learning, growing, and developing go hand in glove with purpose. If you are unclear on your purpose, simply focus on the barriers and challenges that confront you. If you are clear on your sense of purpose, hold on tight—the learning and growing will come fast and furious as long as you keep your eye on your ultimate aim. In Shane's case, his higher purpose caused him to face himself by engaging fully at work. This engagement caused his world view to shift and his skill base to expand.

We've seen others grow as a result of purposeful engagement. As Stan clarified his purpose in Chapter 3, he needed to learn a whole host of new skills, from fund-raising to writing to public speaking. Marsha learned new assessment, relationship, and service skills as a stockbroker. Marilyn learned about what really mattered to her, and Derek learned new management skills. We find life more exciting when we begin living with purpose. Life is more exciting and rewarding because of the increased integrity, the constant learning, and the rapid growing. We are developing our gifts, our capacities. In addition to these qualities, people living with a clear purpose sense a unity in their lives that adds to their fulfillment. **(AMP)***

UNITY

Clear purpose turns our warring interests into powerful teammates.

Purpose encompasses all of our life. Gandhi's actions were not simply political—his principles of non-violence and respect compelled a total lifestyle change. The ashram he developed was a community based on these principles. Gandhi's marriage, his parenting, and all his other relationships were affected by his stance. What started as a political action became an all-encompassing quest that included work, family, and Spirit. A true, higher life purpose unifies all of our life.

As Stan developed his purpose around the value of life, he realized he needed to value his own life fully. That meant time with his children, his friends, and himself. His clarified sense of purpose led him to more service of others and himself. His integrity required that every aspect of his own quality of life come under scrutiny and receive greater attention.

Ellis provided an example of how purpose gives meaning to our activities as well as enhancing performance. He moved from the limited purpose of making money and becoming famous to a greater purpose of serving clients and helping them succeed. The same thing happened in his personal life as he became more invested in ensuring success for his wife, children, friends, community, and extended family.

---

* AMP 1—Think of a new position or attitude that led you to learning. What was that like?

AMP 2—Identify an experience where a renewed sense of purpose led to your learning and growing. What new skills or knowledge areas did you develop? How did you grow as a person?

Ellis's family began functioning much more effectively. His conflicts with his wife decreased as he became more committed to her satisfaction. His children began enjoying him more as he became a better disciplinarian and coach. Ellis's enthusiasm for life manifested itself everywhere. He felt happier than he had ever dreamed possible. He was "on purpose" with his world.

Higher purpose, by definition, encompasses our entire lives. It gives meaning to everything we do, and this common meaning unifies all we do. Sometimes this unification means dropping elements that do not add powerfully to our purpose. We saw this in our consideration of G. D. Searle, which needed to divest itself of divisions that were not "on purpose" in order to refocus. On an individual level, we saw Marsha drop a number of her sales practices as she moved from being a hunter to being a partner with her investors.

Whether we enhance the meaning in what we are doing or let go of "off purpose" activities, a clearer sense of purpose is inclusive and energizing to all purposeful activities in which we engage.

PURPOSE IS DEEPLY PERSONAL

Jazz comes from who you are, where you've been, what you've done. If you don't live it, it won't come out of your horn.

...CHARLIE PARKER

Purpose is deeply personal, employing our gifts and helping us learn the lessons we need to learn in life. Often these lessons result from deficiencies or wounds from earlier in our life.

We've seen how Ellis wanted money and fame. Behind his desire for money and fame was a lifelong sense of being an outsider. This early experience was painful to him, and whenever the pain became too great, he would tell himself it would all be better when he grew up to be rich and famous. It's no wonder he saw his clients more as a means to an end than as people. It's also no surprise that once he began to care about his clients more, his company took off, and the fame and fortune he yearned for became realities.

Money and fame did not heal him, but the caring and contact he had with his clients, family, and those he supported did. As he moved from outsider to valued partner, his childhood experience was being corrected in the daily operation of his business. Each business success brought the outsider further into the center, healing him through the experience of belonging and mutual caring. The same change took place in the rest of his life.

Similar correction can be seen in supervisors who give support they never got, parents who provide care and understanding they never received, teachers who use patience they always needed, and so on. In each case, purpose is influenced by an inner urge to correct earlier deficits. Sally became a healer once she had healed her body and inner self; Casey became an ideal employee as he dealt with the effects of an alcoholic father and an abusive childhood.

Similarly, our personal attributes or gifts determine the nature of our purpose. In Ellis's case, we see a highly intelligent social scientist who uses his scientific training and creative analytic ability to serve. In Derek's case, his gift of good nature and comfort in groups led his company to creative solutions and more stability. Gandhi used his knowledge of the law, and Sally used her gift of healing.

People who are willing to look within and have the courage to face their earlier experiences are more likely to live deeply fulfilling, purposeful lives. This happens because our purpose has greater meaning in light of the historic circumstances we are correcting.

The same is true of our gifts. An honest self-assessment of our strengths and weaknesses helps teach us who we are and where we are going. This honest inventory adds to meaning, because we maximize our gifts and learn new skills where necessary. **(AMP)***

---

* AMP—Explore how an earlier emotional wound has influenced your life direction. How has success in this direction helped heal the wound? Are there gifts you have not developed?

RECIPROCITY AND BALANCE

Even the camel needs water to cross the desert.

Another element common to purpose statements is reciprocity. We must give and receive, or we develop an unbalanced system in which we are drained. In Western culture, we are trained to view purpose as sacrifice, a shortcoming of the Protestant ethic and numerous other scarcity-based cultures around the world. Scarcity beliefs are founded on a belief in limitation as opposed to abundance.

If we give but never receive, we are drained. Even the saintly, giving Mother Teresa, who ministers to countless needy children, would probably tell you that God replenishes her through the service she delivers, she probably feels she receives as much as or more than she gives. Our purpose relates us to the world through mutual service and learning. If it is not mutual, it is out of balance. If it is out of balance, we will be less effective in what we are doing.

In each of the examples of purposeful living we have discussed, there is enormous return for significant investment. This is reciprocity. This is how we get the lessons and energy to deliver the service and teaching we give. Stan experiences a greater sense of self-worth, Ellis is healed as he serves, Casey grows as he participates, and on and on. Purpose must be a two-way street in order to be fully realized.

Rachel

Rachel was an idealist when she entered medical school. Upon graduation, she was even more committed to her ideals of universal health care. She took a low-paying job and regularly worked sixty to ninety hours a week as an internist in a community family-practice clinic.

Over the years, she became more and more dissatisfied as her list of criticisms of the "system" grew longer and longer. She was becoming a chronic complainer, and she was suffering from severe burnout. She had much of what we look for in a life of purpose but lacked the reciprocity. She served fully, but she was not served fully in return.

Out of frustration, she took a staff position at a county hospital and began earning a better wage. Her hours at work tapered off, and she replaced the new time with activity on the county health board. She was not only making more money but also helping more people and positively influencing the system she so bitterly criticized. With some reciprocity, the effectiveness of her mission was increasing, because she was able to help more and more people through policy setting and activism. She still worked as much but was better reimbursed in fiscal, psychological, emotional, and spiritual ways.

Service for Rachel was no longer a matter of "opening a vein" for direct transfusion of her life force to others. Service had grown instead into a full, balanced sense of purpose, and it had become a reciprocal, nourishing, mutual activity—she served and grew as she was better served. Purpose is rarely best fulfilled by sacrifice.

Reciprocity can be out of balance in the other direction, too. Who hasn't worked with someone who takes more than he or she gives? Carl, in Chapter 2, was one such person, who avoided work at all costs but received a substantial salary. Rob took from his firm until Hannah put a stop to it. This kind of imbalance can be especially debilitating to individuals and to the corporations who employ them. There is no positive motivation to give meaning and fulfillment through daily service. Taking is the major end. The give and take of higher purpose is unknown to people operating out of balance in this way.

VISION

> *Where there is no vision, a people perish.*
> ...RALPH WALDO EMERSON

Vision is common to those courageous people who dream and make their dreams reality. Purpose clarifies and generates vision.

Vision is the imagined outworking of purpose. It is what we see on the projection screen when we imagine how purpose will play out in the future.

Purpose is like the slide, life is like the light, and the image on the screen is vision, or projected purpose. Gandhi had a vision of a more egalitarian South Africa, of a free unified India, of a country that operated under principles of respect and democracy. With vision, Ellis developed a clearer sense of vision for his clients. In serving them, he holds that sense of vision, developing products that helped his clients be all that they can be. Ellis develops a clear sense of his clients' potential often beyond what they can imagine. Likewise, his vision for his family expanded. His marriage became something beyond what he had imagined with increasing intimacy and partnership. His parenthood became a process of increasing mutuality and reciprocal contribution with his children. He ultimately sees an entire world operating from justice and compassion for all its members. You could say that he has long term and short term vision. Ellis' vision includes profitable companies that he serves. It includes companies where the communication is open and honest and the teamwork is focused on higher purpose.

Vision is more fluid than purpose which is the more rarefied abstraction. Taking our slide projector analogy further, our circumstances change and the vision changes but the purpose remains the same. Just as variation in the screen or the intensity of light will change the way that a picture looks in slide projection, variations in our life circumstances cause our vision to vary. New resources cause us to shift our ideas and changes in scenario cause use to alter our plans—maintaining at all times constancy of purpose.

Vision can also be understood as purpose projected into our future. It plays a major role in the beacon like quality that purpose serves. It is what we see in our mind's eye. It results from the interaction between purpose and the environment. It manifests as the superior creativity and problem solving that we discussed in Chapter 2. In reading this book, you are developing your own life vision. First, you are developing an idea of what purpose means and ultimately, of your own purpose. In the next chapter, you will develop your purpose statement and after that you will be encouraged to take that purpose into an expanding vision of the potential of your life through the individual and corporate principles of purpose. Today Stan has a vision of a society that values life. He sees his job as honoring, cherishing, and fully developing the life that flows through him in the form of education and well-being for members of our society, and honoring of life on the planet through environmental stewardship.

This vision guides him and is the stuff of which he speaks and with which he deals. His vision of a responsible stewardship causes him to communicate to political decision makers. His vision of a society honoring life causes him to take resolute stands with the legal institutions to put appropriate costs and penalties on those who diminish the quality of life for others.

Casey began with a reactive vision; keeping the perceived enemy at bay. When he clarified his purpose he began generating a creative vision of a successful, friendly corporation. He changed purpose or slides and the picture shifted dramatically.

Purpose generated vision caused Marsha to shift her way of doing business and it created a touchstone of integrity that helped Hannah sort her way through the bad faith of Rob.

Develop your purpose and your vision will sharpen. Learn to live by the principles of purpose and it will come into even finer focus and usefulness.

We will now summarize the essence of purpose—that essential element from which the vision flows—and then take the next step towards helping each of us develop a clear life vision.

In summary, we have seen that purpose:

- is a *natural capacity* of all human beings
- fosters *integrity* or wholeness
- both results from and causes *learning and growing*
- *unifies* all of our life

- flows from *deeply personal* unfinished business and gifts
- causes *reciprocal benefit* to us and our world
- generates *vision* to guide us to our highest

Now we will move on to follow several individuals as they develop their own clearly articulated purpose statements. Then you will have an opportunity to go through the process yourself.

Chapter 5

Developing Your Purpose Statement

A purpose statement is a useful tool. I keep one on my desk in front of me at work most of the time. It motivates me and helps me make decisions. It acts like a tuning fork to help me determine which course of action is most "on purpose." With it, I compare courses of action to select which is most "in tune" with my purpose. My purpose statement often inspires me to take action and risks I might otherwise avoid. By reminding me why I am doing what I am doing, it encourages me and recalls my larger connections.

Developing a purpose statement requires labeling the most rarefied of abstractions. It can be likened to naming the wind—calm to gale, out of the north or south, hot or dry. These phrases describe a phenomenon we call the wind, but they are not the wind. Purpose statements similarly indicate direction for our lives, identify values, and describe our relationship to the world around us. They are not our purpose but help indicate the direction of our purpose, as a telltale hangs from the mast indicating wind direction for sailors. With our purpose statement, we orient our decision-making, just as the sailor trims the sails in relation to the telltale as it is blown by the wind. Similarly, our purpose statement helps us know where we are going and how we are going to get there, the way a compass and map are used by explorers navigating unknown terrain.

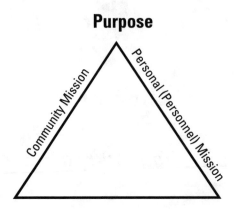

Figure 5.1

FOR INDIVIDUALS

The purpose statement reflects individual values, needs, and gifts so we can apply them in service, self-development, and interaction with the world around us. Our life purpose consists of our personal and community missions. A personal mission consists of the learning, growing, and other personal development experiences in which we engage at any one time and throughout our lives. Our community mission refers to the goods and services we render to others in our lives—from distant, unknown beneficiaries to immediate family. Work can be included here, or imagined as a third mission unto itself.

PERSONAL MISSION + COMMUNITY MISSION = LIFE PURPOSE

In Chapter 4, we read about Rachel as she discovered and developed her purpose as a physician. Rachel's community mission was clear. She intended to bring universal health care to her community in order to alleviate suffering, raise people's living standards, and, ultimately, enhance their enjoyment of life. It was in the realm of her personal mission that she was cloudy. She had made the mistake of so many service personnel—forgetting to include her own benefit, avoiding her own suffering, raising her own standard of living, and enjoying her own life fully. She had not discovered the reciprocity of personal and community mission.

Prior to learning about the power of purpose, her original personal mission statement could have read "to burn myself out in the service of health care to the community." She would never have acknowledged this, but it reflects how she acted. Her revised purpose statement might have read "to live the healthiest possible life with a high standard of living and full enjoyment, so I can develop my gifts to their fullest and practice medicine, helping others limit suffering, raise their own standard of living, and enjoy their lives fully." In this statement we see a clear purpose, consisting of a personal mission statement and a community mission statement.

> *Personal Mission*: To live the healthiest possible life with a high standard of living and full enjoyment, so I can develop my gifts to their fullest.
>
> *Community Mission*: To practice medicine, helping others limit suffering, raise their own standard of living, and enjoy their lives fully.

Not all life purpose statements will have a profession designated, but well-balanced statements will be reciprocal and define our relationship to our community. By reciprocal, we mean a two-way benefit. Rachel's original statement lacked reciprocity—in it, she was drained in the service of others. It was like she opened a vein to give blood with no infusion to her in return. Her revised statement required reciprocity, a two-way benefit, in which she was nourished rather than drained as she served.

Her purpose statement meets another requirement. It is never-ending and continues beyond her work career. Legendary Alabama football coach Bear Bryant clearly had a mission limited by football, and he died within a year of retiring, as he had predicted. His "reason for living" was complete. Another example of limited purpose is the "empty-nest" syndrome in which parents become lost in life or depressed, without their children to live for. Once retired, Rachel can continue in her life purpose without practicing medicine, by serving grandchildren, her community, and so on.

A clearly articulated purpose statement might have helped Rachel change her clinic or move to another practice setting sooner. She would have seen that reciprocity was missing and adjusted accordingly. Learning the lesson the way Rachel did, however, was "on purpose." She needed to learn that the "open vein" transmission to humanity was "off purpose"—that self-sacrifice is seldom "on purpose" except in rare cases like war. Self sacrifice often is a misguided attempt to heal old wounds like the overprotective parent who felt unloved as a child and over-does the show of affection to their own offspring. Lessons, not sacrifice, generally define our path. A path is the route we follow to our highest purpose. Self-sacrifice is often simply un-creative problem solving, which perpetuates limits rather than correcting them. Learning these lessons could be said to be part of Rachel's path, indicated by her purpose.

PERSONAL AND COMMUNITY MISSION

A complete purpose statement reflects our likes, abilities, and values as they come to focus in our ultimate life aim. To arrive at statements of our personal and community missions, we make a personal inventory of our affinities, capacities, values, and ulti-mate concerns. We also include reflections on these by others.

Our *affinities* are our likes—the things we are drawn to. They can be simple, everyday pleasures like smelling flowers or having a clean house. They can be larger enjoyments like build-ing organizations, influencing opinions, or raising a family.

Our *capacities* are things we do easily or well. They may be developed or undeveloped. They include skills, beneficial char-acteristics, and personal traits. Skills are things we can do, and characteristics or traits include height, appearance, personality, and drive.

Values refer to the attitudes, actions, and activities such as occupations we hold in high esteem, whether we see them as strong in ourselves or others. Values are things we find important and respect.

Our *ultimate concerns* are the overarching values by which we appraise our entire life. They are closely linked to our ultimate life purpose, because it is in living them fully that our life purpose is fulfilled.

Reflections refers to the value others see in us: what they like, respect, or admire about us. Frequently others see our affinities, capacities, qualities, values, and ultimate concerns more objectively and clearly than we do.

THE LIFE PURPOSE STATEMENT

Our life purpose is generally revealed to us as we live our lives. At different times, different life purpose statements can bring our purpose to focus. The statement can be simple or complex. There is no "right" way to articulate purpose, but certain characteristics can enhance a purpose statement's usefulness. The statement should move you deeply. The attunement can be so right, it often brings tears of fullness and joy as people discover it.

In the chapter on common characteristics of life purpose, we saw that purpose is a *natural capacity* that fosters *integrity* and promotes *learning and growing*. It *unifies* our lives from a *deeply personal* foundation and is *reciprocal* in nature.

Purpose statements can be simple: "I live to love and be loved"; "I create art so I can experience and share beauty"; "I help my friends and employees succeed so I can live a successful life." They can be complex: "I learn and grow in my professional life as an attorney and in my personal life as a father, husband, and community member so I can serve fully and help others succeed in their highest purposes." Generally, it can be boiled down to one sentence. If it goes longer, it well may be a vision statement, which is a more detailed articulation of a purpose statement as it manifests in our consciousness and circumstances at a given time.

Each of the above purpose statements provides a touchstone in daily activity. I can ask myself which alternative or direction is more loving, beautiful, successful or enriching if those are values articulated in my purpose statement. A strong purpose statement aids in daily discernment. Note that each statement given has a value like love, beauty, success, or growth. Each is reciprocal, leads to learning and growth, and enhances integrity and service. Notice how each of the statements has both a personal and a community mission.

PERSONAL	**COMMUNITY**
I live to be loved.	I love (others).
I create art to experience beauty.	I share beauty.
I help so I can live a successful life.	I help my friends and employees succeed.
I learn and grow in my professional and personal life.	I serve fully and help others succeed in their highest purpose.

Let's examine a few people's experiences as they articulated their life purpose statements. You will have an opportunity to develop a statement for yourself at the end of the chapter. Look ahead or start jotting down notes if you wish. **(AMP)****

STAN

We saw in Chapter 3 how Stan's life purpose evolved. Now we will take a look at how he developed his fully articulated purpose statement. First he attended a workshop on life purpose that began much the way this book has begun. That seminar

---

* AMP—Start playing with possible aspects of your personal and community mission statements. Don't worry about whether they are the truly right or best statements. Just create as many possible ideas as you can. You might want to jot them down separately or at the end of this chapter in the blanks supplied.

presented the benefits of focusing our lives on higher purpose and then reviewed the common elements of living purpose. Exercises followed in which each participant developed a personal purpose statement.

Life Review And Gleaning

In exploring his *ultimate concern*, he completed three exercises. The first was an eyes-closed review of his life, to fill in affinities, capacities, reflections, and values. In this review of his life, starting with the most recent events and going back to his birth in five-year increments, he was to look for what mattered most to him as well as scanning for life lessons, wounds, and unfinished business.

Stan's life unrolled before him, and he saw many choices he had made from values he considered hollow. He liked much of who he was in his day-to-day life but questioned the larger decisions. He saw himself as a little boy alone in various foreign countries around the world. Nor did he find the warmth for which he yearned. He'd grown up with a mother whose ultimate concerns seemed to him to be acquiring wealth and being accepted by hiding from neighbors her ethnic identity. He figured that this was an important part of his overemphasized value on financial success. Financial success meant self-worth and acceptance to him. It also led him to undervalue love, relationships, and just living life well.

Life, as he learned in childhood, was a puzzle to be figured out so money could be amassed. This was the imagined road to ultimate security. He became sad at the limited, unappreciative nature of this. He wanted to be loved and valued for who he was, not only for what he could earn. His ex-wife had initially been attracted to him because of money, and he learned the hard way how hollow that could be. Numerous other scenes of pain and victory followed. His life lesson seemed to include valuing himself unconditionally, expressing himself genuinely, recognizing and caring for his own needs, and learning to trust and serve others.

The first thing Stan did after his review was list his *affinities*, or the things he liked doing. This led him to consider a wide range of likes, including travel, meeting people, solving problems, raising his children, running, loving, public speaking, helping people, serving others, writing, competing, and reading.

Next, he explored his *capacities*, the things he did well. He'd been blessed with good health, excellent physical abilities, a razor-sharp mind, strong debating ability, good analytic skills, a top economics education, great friends, good problem-solving abilities, a strong sense of honor, and the ability to tell a joke well.

For *reflection*, he turned to friends who said he was bold, caring, loyal, determined, supportive, steadfast, and a host of other attributes, all of which he found uncomfortable. These were among his highest values, the things he'd lacked but yearned for as a child. He was moved and embarrassed to learn that others saw them in him.

The things he *respected* or found *valuable in others* included courage, ingenuity, creativity, willingness to go against the flow, loving, support, success, honesty, and devotion.

Deathbed Scene

Next, he imagined his life going forward to his deathbed. He asked himself whom he would want to be there with him when he died and what he would need to be able to say in order to feel he had fulfilled his life purpose and let go of his life. This inquiry helped him clarify his ultimate concern, which was to be able to say he had lived and loved as fully as he could and that his friends, family, and society had benefited from his time on earth. He found himself crying at these thoughts. He was both sad and happy: sad that he had lived so much of his life forgetting the importance of this and happy that he had the rest of his life to focus on what was ultimately important to him.

Following this, he completed a final inventory by writing his own epitaph and obituary as he wished it would be written. He arrived at a final statement that surprised him, since wealth was not central. It stated, "Here lies Stan—a man who learned his lessons, lived and loved fully, and was well loved." He knew this was the truth—that this reflected his ultimate concern. Whereas his deathbed scenario brought tears to his eyes, this exercise was extremely sobering. He was beginning to feel a determination stirring deep within him that he loved. He was feeling focused and strong. None of the usual social concerns about acceptance, approval, and wealth that drove him were present.

Individuals in the workshop were then told to review all they had written, circling the elements that resonated with them most deeply or that they felt the strongest about or yearned for the most. Stan found this much easier than he expected. The last two exercises had given him a perspective that made the job flow.

He then reviewed, in more depth, the life traumas, wounds, learnings, themes, and unfinished business that influenced his ultimate concerns and purpose. He figured that his family's shame about being different religiously was one element of his self-rejection and that self-acceptance was a necessary part of his path. His mother's concern about money over relationship, even with him, seemed to be a hurt and a hurdle on his way to self-acceptance. Learning to love and be loved seemed to be a critical part of his unfinished business, along with the need to learn self-nourishment and self-worth. Using his talents fully in the service of humanity seemed to Stan to be part of loving fully.

These all seemed to come together for him in his concern about the value of life. He knew that a shift in values was part of his life lesson. He felt he needed to learn to value all of God's creation, starting with himself. Learning to value life personally seemed to be a first step toward helping others do so. Fortuitously, it had already presented itself as a concern and activity in his life.

He and other participants then began experimenting with personal and community mission statements, looking for the ones that spoke to them most strongly and represented most clearly the realities of their present lives. They were encouraged to look for threads that ran through their personal inventories to see what they were good at, liked, and respected in others as a reflection of their highest selves. They asked friends to help them fill in their blind spots and did a final check on their mission statements with others. Stan's community mission statement was to alleviate human suffering by helping individuals learn from suffering, and complete their unfinished business in traumatic losses, letting go of resentments, learning their lessons, and moving on; in general, to help others appreciate fully the value of life so they could live the fullest lives possible no matter what trauma had befallen them. His personal mission was to learn to live his highest values, growing in self-acceptance and the ability to love his children and friends fully so he could become the happiest, most loving person possible.

Then he and the rest of the group combined their two mission statements and shared these with each other in small groups. Sobs could be heard around the room as participants were moved by the strength of their yearning to live true to their highest.

Stan was one of the first to share his ultimate purpose statement with the whole group. He glowed as he stood to begin, but his face contorted with tears and sobs as he declared that his life purpose was to learn to love himself fully by learning to love others as they learned together to live life fully and value life in all its aspects. When asked what the tears were about, he said that he felt he was changing already, since this wasn't as important-sounding as he would have liked. In fact, he had never wanted anything more than to be loved, but that had never seemed okay or impressive enough. His sobbing increased as he told how he had never felt good enough for his father or mother, so he'd concluded he was unworthy. He could now see that his lesson was clearly to learn to love himself and help others do the same. His community mission to help others learn to value life as an economist stemmed directly from his own deepest need. He'd never felt the connection so deeply before.

When you develop your own purpose statement, the deeper you can look into your past and the more courageously

you can view your historic pains, the more meaningful and personal you will find your purpose statement to be. The depth of
Stan's experience is fairly common for people of all occupations,
walks of life, and levels of worldly responsibility. Cabdrivers,
CEOs, secretaries, salesmen, housewives—anyone from any
walk of life is likely to feel this level of guiding, motivating
power in an accurate, heartfelt purpose statement.

CASEY

We met Casey in Chapter 3, where we saw how his clarity of
purpose helped him run his warehouse in harmony with others
to fulfill the company's ultimate purpose. We saw how fear originally drove his vigilance. He was reticent at the beginning of
the exercise to discover his higher purpose. His self-esteem was
pretty low, and he feared he would come up blank. His memory
of past failures and firings was resurrected—he said he'd rather
stick his tongue in a light socket than go through it.

He was surprised at how peaceful and sad he felt in his life
review. He began relaxing when he started listing his likes.
Sports headed the list and led him to reflect that he also liked
working in teams. He liked finding and fixing problems and being a "heads-up" competitor. He liked women and horsing
around. Dancing was fun, and so was meeting deadlines the
other guys thought were impossible.

He started to be afraid of listing his capacities until he
thought of his last review at work—where his boss told him he
was the most dependable shipping and warehouse manager
they'd ever had. He wasn't the best at establishing systems, but
he was absolutely committed to following them. He realized he
was also good at helping his team succeed. He would even go to
a guy's house to make sure he got to work on time when things
weren't going so well for him.

The reflection exercise was a revelation when he heard
friends say he was steadfast, kind, hardworking, and fun to be
with. One guy even said he'd rather have Casey covering his
back on a dangerous mission than anyone else he knew.

Casey's values as reflected by those he respected were honesty, hard work, caring, and intelligence. He liked leaders with enthusiasm and team members who did what they were supposed to do. He also respected people who were rebellious and could take necessary, unpopular, irreverent stands with authority.

Casey figured his biggest unfinished business was self-acceptance. His parents' overprotectiveness helped him see himself as incompetent, while their brutality caused him to think there was something wrong with him. Self-criticism seemed to be his biggest stumbling block, along with debilitating shame. He knew he'd grown in self-acceptance and liked the idea of getting even better at it, because he knew it made him better at work and in friendship.

His other life lessons seemed to focus on respecting himself, trusting others, and creating what he most yearned for: a loving circle of friends and family. He felt that his work lessons were to take self-acceptance into stronger leadership, camaraderie, and service to the company and its customers.

Casey's ultimate concerns, as reflected in his deathbed scenario and obituary, were to be valued and loved by his friends and family as much as he loved and valued them. His obituary statement was, "He was a good member of God's team, loving, learning, and laughing fully. He was loved by those who knew him. He will be missed by friends and family."

As Casey began circling the items that mattered most to him, he saw trustworthiness, teams, and service as central to his life. He also felt that caring and support were important. His community mission was to serve honestly and lovingly to the best of his ability in the areas of work, friendship, family, and his community. His personal mission seemed summed up by self-acceptance and, ultimately, learning to love others as fully as he loved himself.

Before reading his purpose statement, he told the group how much he had gotten out of it. His life didn't seem like a waste anymore. He could clearly see that he pulled his weight and that he would never again be the same defensive guy who got fired three times for hostility and insubordination.

He saw as his purpose in life, to do his best wherever he was, to care for his friends and coworkers, and with them to do the job they had to do to the best of their ability, so they could play their part on God's team. Casey's community mission is clearly stated above, but his personal mission is harder to see. The reciprocity in Casey's statement is in loving and being loved: he doesn't talk about self-acceptance directly, but love represented this to him.

ELIZABETH

Elizabeth graduated with an MBA from one of the most respected schools on the east coast. She went to work for a top New York ad agency in account management straight out of school. Her work was so strong that her main account soon hired her away, making her the youngest director of marketing for a Fortune 500 company. The company doubled its size during her tenure, before she was lured to Chicago to become vice president of marketing for another firm interested in growing like Elizabeth's previous firm had.

Elizabeth looked forward eagerly to the life purpose statement development exercise. She'd had a sense of mission since her childhood in Trenton, New Jersey. As the oldest of five children of alcoholic parents, she had early in life realized her budding mission as she felt compelled to protect her brothers and sisters. She was cooking and cleaning by eight and working outside the house from twelve on. She felt a sense of purpose not only at home but also in school, where she sang in the choir and starred in school musicals and plays. For her, going to church felt purposeful, for it was there that she "talked to God" about all her concerns.

She knew she was gifted and felt certain she had received so much for a reason. Her list of likes went on and on, including her love of problem solving, creating, talking to people, and homemaking—like cooking and sewing. She liked spending time with her husband, singing in the church choir, camping, hunting, and fishing.

The capacity inventory she wrote was similarly enthusiastic and voluminous. She was good at quantitative analysis but preferred qualitative. She wrote, sang, planned, and solved problems well. She seemed to be a strong team leader and saw herself as a good strategist. One of the things that had always intrigued her was why she had been given so much talent.

Reflection was especially rewarding for her, since siblings and friends had been so important in her life. They told her things she longed to hear—that she was determined, driving, loving, relentless, understanding, gracious, and wonderfully supportive. They respected her integrity and courage in the face of tough stands that could lead to rejection.

Her values were intelligence, courage, determination, devotion, service, and love. Heroes she looked to were Albert Schweitzer, Marie Curie, Gandhi, Jonas Salk, Thomas Jefferson, and John Paul Jones. She discovered, as do so many, that what she valued in others was a reflection of herself.

Elizabeth spent a good deal of time reviewing what she called holes in her childhood—she said they made her life look like Swiss cheese to her, with strong, solid areas of "cheese" and big holes of need. In addition to the unfinished business of her childhood, she felt the need to develop compassion for those in authority and others who don't meet her standards. Her intolerance of what she called "corporate leadership incompetence" reduced her effectiveness in work considerably, turning her marketing departments into islands rather than integrated units. She understood that her authority issues included problems with control, since she resented any uninvited incursions into her domain, no matter how harmless or appropriate. If she hadn't been so talented, she believed she'd have been fired long before.

Her ultimate concerns were to contribute to the world and be loved by her husband and children. She envisioned an epitaph that said, "She played hard, loved fully, and was a blessing to all."

She found it difficult to pick among her qualities until she thought about her ultimate benefactor: God. Then she picked the ones that seemed to come from or bring her closer to the deity. Her purpose statement then took form: "To use the gifts God has given me to heal, develop, and use myself so that I can serve fully for the healing and development of all those I encounter, especially my family, friends, and coworkers."

We see here a fully developed purpose statement with a personal mission to heal, develop, and use the gifts God has given her. Her community mission is to use those gifts to help others heal and develop. She might have added more reciprocity by looking more to her own development, but including her own "healing" is a step in the right direction.

ED

Ed was a bank turnaround artist. He had taken numerous financial institutions around the world from losing to winning big in a few years. His frugal Midwest German roots proved invaluable in cutting away corporate fat and developing good systems. One of his strongest attributes was his willingness to let go of bad business. He showed unusual courage in his willingness to lose money early in a turnaround. He let go of what he called "weak money" and high maintenance low benefit clients in order to solidify his base for strong growth moves in the years that followed. His vice presidents of sales and marketing invariably fought with him through the first year or two of a turnaround, until they saw the positive effects of his policies.

He had a similar reputation as a board member for various funds and financial institutions. He could read a balance sheet and diagnose problems with uncanny insight and accuracy. Deals he brokered almost always succeeded, since his due diligence was both uncommonly courageous in identifying possibilities and unusually thorough in identifying weaknesses of potential investments and acquisitions.

In listing his likes, he thought first of how he liked to develop staff. He was especially proud of the worldwide community of his former employees. He liked cooperative, winning teams, the opera, church, golf, and sex. He loved reading the classics, especially never-ending Russian novels. He liked both a fast ski and simply sitting and praying in his flower garden. He loved his daughters and their success, and he liked vacations with them.

Capacities for him seemed to blend with his likes. He was good with numbers, planning, staff development, and marketing. He learned languages quickly and was good at cross-cultural deals. He was a strong competitor and a devoted partner. As he looked at it, he found he was good at most things in banking but felt at a loss to identify skills outside work.

Reflection by others helped him identify skills outside of work—friends told him he was caring, versatile, quick-witted, pleasant, helpful, and supportive. They reminded him about his beautiful voice and devoted service to his church. He was taken aback by his blindness in this sphere.

He valued integrity, tenacity, follow-through, initiative, intelligence, and courage in others. He reported enjoying this exercise as he reviewed not only historic and literary heroes he emulated but also present and past employees he respected and valued.

Unfinished business for him seemed to flow from his sense of his family's strengths, which he saw as their weaknesses too. He was lonely as a leader. His perfectionism made life much less enjoyable. He always "needed to drive" and felt he needed to learn to go along for the ride more and to allow others a chance to catch up and take more responsibility. He clearly needed to "smell the roses." He found he was a better boss and father than husband and yearned for more cooperation and closeness with his wife.

His deathbed scene was peopled with family, friends, and former employees he had mentored. He wanted to say that he had served his employers, family, and coworkers to his utmost with loyalty and care and that they were all richer for his having been in their lives.

Ed balked at his obituary until he heard some of the others. Self-praise was very difficult for him, yet he acknowledged that praise and recognition were personal drivers. He finally decided he wanted his obituary to read, "The community has lost a loving employer, father, and citizen who left us all richer for having known, worked with, and been loved by him."

Ed's purpose statement read as follows: "It is my purpose to serve others professionally and personally in banking and wealth building so that they may know greater abundance and security; so that I can grow in security within myself, discovering God's riches and celebrating life with my family, friends, coworkers and others."

You may have noted that Ed's is the only example that mentions a specific vocation in his community mission statement. He felt a strong affinity to his profession, as do many artists, healers, and other professionals, who see "the stuff" of their career as central to their mission. It doesn't really matter whether you are specific in this way or not, as long as you are moved, inspired, and focused by your statement.

TWO WHO DIDN'T

Not everyone arrives readily at a deep, meaningful life purpose statement. In my experience, there are two main reasons for this. One is a lack of self-reflection. The other is perhaps more problematic. It is when the individual has moved radically "off purpose" and a clear, genuine articulation of purpose would threaten this position, requiring radical change beyond this person's capabilities or, more generally, his or her desire.

Ben

Ben owned a chain of restaurants in suburban Milwaukee. He started them with Zeke, his partner, when they were both fresh out of college. They were the "bachelor" entrepreneurs about town, with women galore, riding the wave of chic theme restaurants from the late '70s into the '80s.

Their service was the best, and their food was tops. They carried both vegetarian and meat dishes and their recipes were innovative, so they were big with a wide range of customers.

Marriage seemed to be their downfall. They didn't add another restaurant to the business after their weddings. Ben believed his partner, Zeke, was being pulled away from the business by his wife, and he began resenting Zeke's half share of the firm's income. Each of them was responsible for three operations, and Zeke's were not doing as well as his. Their fighting was bitter and never-ending. Ben was fighting with his own spouse, too. He ended up divorcing her and pulling out of the partnership with Zeke all in the same year. Zeke offered to buy Ben out or split the businesses, but Ben wouldn't hear of either. If they split, Zeke would "get away" with his partner's share, even though his restaurants weren't doing as well and Zeke would have taken the weaker part of the business. If Zeke bought the business, Ben was certain he would run the whole thing into the ground and forfeit the balance of the payments.

Ben refused Zeke's offer to buy him out and made a counteroffer. Zeke refused until Ben's offer was so high that his bankers advised Ben against it. The deal looked so bad to Ben's bank, in fact, that they demanded a personal guarantee and would cover only fifty percent of the amount, leaving Ben to borrow the balance from friends and Zeke.

Good business had nothing to do with Ben's reasoning. Revenge was his main motivation—revenge on his wife and Zeke. This was his way to "show them." Neither Zeke nor anyone else was clear what he or she was being shown—Ben's wife walked away with a nice settlement, and Zeke retired to Marina del Rey, California, living harborside, where he could consult when he wanted or "roll out of bed into his boat" to fish, water ski, or simply cruise.

The harder Ben pushed, the worse the business seemed to perform. He could never get the right managers in Zeke's places and closed two of them within a year and a half. His banker was rightfully concerned, since Ben consistently seemed to make bad decisions. When Ben finally came to Chicago to get help, things were really bad. Only one of his four remaining restaurants was in the black, and it simply couldn't make up for the others.

While discussing his life purpose, Ben began crying—he couldn't articulate one. He never completed the exercises, and when he was walked through them, he couldn't even fake it. He'd become so driven by hate and bitterness that the thought of his higher purpose caused him great anxiety. He terminated the consulting relationship. Within two years, he had defaulted on his loans and was seeking refinancing.

Ben's story, sadly, is not unusual. When we've gotten ourselves into something for the wrong reasons and don't want to look them in the face, then life purpose seems like an indictment. Most of us get stubborn about certain off-purpose moves also and wait too long to react. Ben found the unfinished business and life lessons part of the exercise impossible. As far as he was concerned, his problems were due to his ex-wife and partner. He was so devastated by the loss of the two most important people in his life that he refused to consider questions of ultimate concern because of the pain it evoked.

He finally concluded that the exercises were stupid and useless—changes in the market were clearly at the root of his problems. What he needed was to update the restaurants. He seemed either incapable or unwilling to face his responsibility in his unhappiness and, failing this, couldn't move ahead.

Marge

Marge was CEO of an American greeting card company owned by a British firm. In her mid-forties, she had been with the company her entire working career. She knew nothing else and was as high in the company as she could go. The parent company did not bring nonfamily members into responsible positions at the corporate level, and at any rate, she had no desire to move to England.

Marge's two children had found her last relocation to the headquarters city especially difficult, mostly because of her husband's discontent and difficulty finding a new position. She promised the family she wouldn't move again until the kids were out of high school—in six years at the earliest. Marge also knew that she and her husband had a tendency to drink too much—she had tried to quit several times, with no more than a few months' success.

Work had become routine and uninspiring. Behind her back, staff complained of her unavailability and her hypocrisy. They felt she "talked the talk but couldn't walk the walk." Marge was known to foster open communication for everyone but herself—anyone who had a problem with her was sent to the employee assistance program or the corporate consultant. She'd earned the title of the Teflon president—no problems ever stuck to her or stopped at her doorstep.

Marge was a strong strategist but lacked vision. As a result, the company was simply going through its paces, growing slowly but never experiencing growth spurts like creative companies with inspired leadership. Marge was going nowhere fast and knew it. When the holding company hired a consultant to do a climate and operations survey she welcomed the input on the surface, even trying to go along with the consultants to the best of her limited ability. That was when the issue of her purpose and mission was raised.

She was great at talking about plans but showed no vision and shied away from personal or corporate discussions of purpose. Part of this was due to her personal situation, and part simply reflected the closed family structure of the parent company. The owners were known as humanitarians, but in truth, they saw their corporations as simple cash cows. Their humanitarian urges reached out to their communities, not to their employees. Employees were paid as little as necessary to fend off unionization in the printing and distribution areas. Just as there was no hope of promotion for Marge, the employees never felt appreciated or encouraged at the highest levels.

Marge developed mission and purpose statements, but they were hollow exercises. She was not honest with herself about her strengths and weaknesses, and she was largely unwilling to look meaningfully at her life lessons and unfinished business. Her alcohol consumption was absolutely off limits for discussion, although she frequently mentioned the need to cut down "because of my extra 10 lbs." Marge's situation is common, but sad nonetheless. She feared the cure for her situation and still sits dissatisfied with her parent company ten years later. The golden handcuffs of position, salary, and alcohol addiction keep her bound in her role as Teflon president. She keeps herself cut off from the mutuality and full power of higher purpose.

An honest self-inventory is essential for a powerful purpose statement. In doing your own inventory, be sure to check with your closest friends. Ask them about your lessons and challenges. Have them help you with your inventory and other steps.

Don't worry about the form. Your statement will evolve over time anyway. Remember, it is only a reflection of your purpose, a tool to bring your purpose to focus in guiding your life, to use in planning, decision making, and managing your energy for the greatest fulfillment and productivity.

Developing Your Life Purpose Statement

(Optional-For a guided audiotape of this process and workbook call 312-645-8300)

A complete purpose statement reflects your likes, abilities, and values as they come to focus in your ultimate life aim. To arrive at your statement of life purpose, you will need to make a personal inventory of your affinities, capacities, values, and ultimate concerns. You will also explore wounds and unfinished business from your past that have influenced your life direction.

Your life purpose statement, a combination of your personal and community mission statements, will be most powerful if it incorporates your most deeply developed preferences, skills, and values. In this exercise you will review your life, looking for factors that have shaped your life and given it direction. These factors include:

- Likes, affinities, and interests: these can include anything from everyday pleasures like having a neat house and enjoying walks to more developed interests like raising a family, building organizations, and writing novels.
- Capacities: the things you do naturally, easily, or well. They may be developed or undeveloped. They include skills, beneficial characteristics, and personal strengths. Skills are things you can do; characteristics or traits include height, appearance, and personality; strengths include drive, persistence, and so on.
- Traumas: the losses, injuries, setbacks, and failures you've experienced. One of the key factors that lead to successful fulfillment of purpose is our ability to recover and learn from setbacks. How we respond to trauma is often critical in determining our ultimate life purpose. As you review your life, explore how you have responded to trauma, what opportunities for growth these experiences have provided, and how these experiences have influenced your life direction.
- Ultimate concerns or values: whatever you most deeply value or hold most dear. These can include abstractions like love or justice as well as tangible objects or specific persons or groups.

Life Review

Step 1. Use the space provided or your own notebook. If you are using your own notebook, separate pages by category by writing the headings *Affinities, Capacities, Traumas,* and *Ultimate Concerns* on individual pages.

Start with your present life situation. Let your mind go over each of the four factor areas in your work, social, personal, family, and spiritual life. Write down as much as you can in each area.

Affinities. Write a list of your affinities. Start with what you currently like doing in your work and personal life. Be sure to include the hobbies, interests, work projects, passions, and whatever you have most enjoyed doing in your life. These may range from everyday pleasures to more developed interests like family, leadership, religious affiliations, and so on.

_____

_____

_____

_____

_____

_____

Capacities. List your capacities, the things you do easily or well. They may be developed or undeveloped. They include skills, beneficial characteristics, and personal strengths. Skills are things you can do; characteristics or traits include height, appearance, and personality; strengths include drive, persistence, and so on.

_____

_____

_____

_____

_____

_____

Traumas. Make a list of traumas you have experienced. Include any losses, injuries, failures, or setbacks you have encountered. Recall how you responded to each situation and how it might have influenced the direction your life has taken. Rate each from 1 to 5, least to most, in terms of the impact it has had on your life.

_____

_____

_____

_____

_____

Ultimate Concerns. List your ultimate concerns and values. Include people, things, abstractions such as love or peace—anything that you treasure and hold very dear.

_____

_____

_____

_____

_____

Once you've completed your current life situation review, go back five years from today and review your life, adding additional information to each category. If you are having trouble recalling things, note job changes, changes in residence, health, friends, weight, and so on, and see what else you might want to add to your lists. Our interests, values, and talents change, so note only changes or additions.

Once that review is completed, continue going back in five-year increments, reviewing your life in detail and noting additions that arise under each category. Write these down. Continue in this way back to your earliest childhood, as early as you can recall or have been told.

Step 2. From your life review, list or circle the three to five likes, affinities, or interests that are most important to you now or that have been most important or formative to your life.

_____

_____

_____

Step 3. List the three to five capacities that are most important for your life now or that have been formative in your life.

_____

_____

_____

Step 4. For a reflection of the *qualities, skills,* and *attributes* others see in you, interview several friends and colleagues about their perceptions of your positive traits in these areas. Take time to let your friends know you are exploring questions related to your life purpose and that you would like their feedback. Then write down their positive reflections, either then or immediately after the meeting.

Step 5. List the qualities or characteristics you most *respect* or *value* in others. The others may be friends, colleagues, heroes, mentors, historical figures you have admired, figures you have studied, and so on.

Step 6. List the major *traumas, losses,* or *failures* in your life. Think about how you have responded to them. What challenges have they presented to you? What opportunities for learning and growth did they provide? How have they influenced your current life direction?

Purpose Fulfillment Statement

Step 7. To begin exploring your ultimate concerns and values, set aside time in a quiet place where you won't be interrupted or disturbed. Begin by taking a few deep breaths and allowing your body to relax. Imagine yourself at the end of your life. You are lying on your deathbed, surrounded by all the people who care most about you and about whom you care most deeply. Imagine yourself in this situation. Take a moment to let yourself get the feel of the situation and clearly picture the scene. Ask yourself what you need to be able to say in order to feel you have fulfilled your life purpose, to be ready to leave your life and your work here. Begin with the phrase, "I have . . . ," and then allow yourself to imagine completing whatever you need to say (include what you have most valued about your life, your most important contributions, your greatest pleasure, and your greatest contribution to others). Write this down.

_____

_____

_____

_____

Once this is done, let yourself "listen" to what you would want to hear from others in order to be ready to leave them. What would you most want to hear? From whom? Allow yourself to "listen" and feel the dialogue as you imagine them speaking to you. Allow yourself to imagine responding to them if that feels right.

After you have completed this dialogue, make any adjustments you wish to the Step 7 purpose fulfillment statement.

Step 8. Write a statement of what you hold to be your *ultimate concern*, based on the deathbed dialogue scene. What values, relationships, accomplishments, and qualities do you hold to be of greatest concern in your life?

_____

_____

_____

_____

Step 9. Write your *epitaph* as you would like it. What would you want written on your tombstone?

_____

_____

_____

Step 10. Write your *obituary* as you would like it to be written. Again, be sure that it reflects your deathbed dialogue scene and your ultimate concerns and values.

_____

_____

_____

Step 11. Review all that you have written in Steps 1 through 10. Circle the elements that resonate most deeply, about which you feel the strongest, or for which you yearn the most. Do not take for granted things you are already doing.

Step 12. Begin writing your personal and community mission statements.

Personal mission statement. Indicate how your affinities, capacities, traumas, and values give focus to your personal life—what you are here to learn, experience, accomplish and how you are intended to benefit. You can include family service here or in a separate statement:

_____

_____

_____

_____

Community mission statement. Indicate how your affinities, capacities, experiences, and values provide focus for your service to others—what you are here to give, serve, and contribute in your work/service life. You can include community service here or in a separate statement:

_____

_____

_____

_____

Step 13. Now bring these two (or four) statements together into a single life purpose statement. Here, it is important that the statement feel all-encompassing and ring true for you and that it genuinely speak to what your life is about. Remember, this is a statement of your *higher* purpose, so don't feel you have to be living true to this statement at all times for it to be valid. It is a statement of how you genuinely want to be living and a call to get back on track when you have fallen off purpose.

Your life purpose statement:

_____

_____

_____

_____

Checklist:

Is your life purpose statement:

- Reciprocal _____
- Growth Promoting _____
- Unifying _____
- Never-ending, ever-expanding _____

Step 14. List the barriers that keep you from living true to your purpose. What limiting values, beliefs, self-defeating behaviors, compulsions, preoccupations, and distractions, keep you off purpose in your life?

If you want more quality information in this area, ask the friends and colleagues you interviewed earlier to give you feedback on what they see. How do they see you getting in your own way or limiting your capacity to live true to your purpose? Share your purpose statement with them to help guide them in their feedback to you.

Summarize your most important barriers or self-limiting behaviors:

LIMITING BEHAVIORS AND BARRIERS	**CORRECTIVE ACTIONS**
_____	_____
_____	_____
_____	_____
_____	_____
_____	_____

Go back and fill in corrective actions you will take to overcome these limits.

Step 15. Remember, no purpose statement is a final product. It needs to be reviewed periodically. Review this statement with your friends and revise it as needed to help you orient to your path throughout your life.

We now move on to guidelines for living your purpose statement daily. (For corporate purpose development examples, see Chapter 9.) Working and living from a perspective of purpose presents many obstacles. We will discuss barriers, pitfalls, and challenges as well as ways to leverage, enhance, and empower performance with purpose.

Chapter 6

Purposeful Living Guidelines

It takes a lifetime to learn how to live.
...JUDITH WRIGHT

Living "on purpose" is a skill. We learn the skill by living life fully, associating with like-minded winning individuals and groups, and learning our lessons, especially the lessons of adversity. We must accept failure, move through our blocks, and allow ourselves no excuses, while at the same time being kind and generous to ourselves. This helps us on the way to self-knowledge which accompanies and fosters the key skill, mastering our mind. All this is facilitated by following the principles of purpose we outline in the next chapter. First, let's examine the dynamics of learning our lessons and keeping "on purpose."

KEEPING ON PURPOSE—BEING ON PURPOSE

Ultimately, everything we do is "on purpose." If we imagine a triangle with purpose at its apex, then everything we do in our lives falls within.

By dropping a line vertically from the ultimate purpose point to the base, we define the line that is "on purpose," or the heart of who we have been, are, and are becoming.

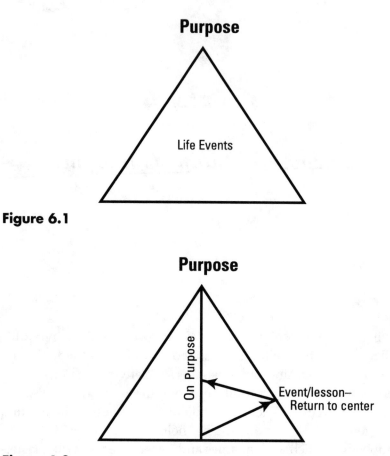

Figure 6.1

Figure 6.2

Early on in our lives, all our interactions with the world were on purpose, no matter how bothersome they were to our parents. Jumping in puddles was fun and taught us about the nature of mothers and water, breaking a glass taught us about glass and gravity, throwing food was the beginning of our mastery of eating and silverware. These movements represent important but often erratic moves in our development of purposeful living.

With each of these movements we learn, change our behavior, and become more developed as human beings. As we act increasingly "on purpose," we focus our energies, and our

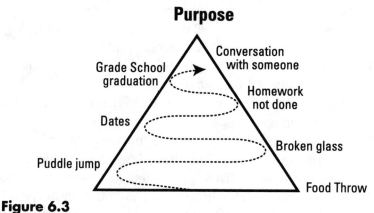

Figure 6.3

movements become less erratic. Our whole life can be seen as a gradual focusing. We adjust course more quickly and expand the triangle forward with more power and velocity toward our ultimate concerns.

Each turn and return to center represents a lesson learned or course adjustment made; for example, "I've learned to jump in puddles only when I don't mind getting wet. I no longer need to read Dick and Jane in order to learn and grow."

Being "off purpose" is a normal part of being "on purpose," just as the innumerable small steering-wheel adjustments we make while driving our car helps us get where we are going.

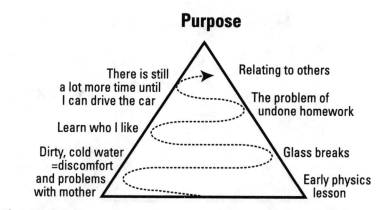

Figure 6.4

Even if we have a mishap, it is still part of our journey. Ideally, we make moves, learn lessons, adjust course, or benefit in some way from all pleasurable and painful experience and then move on.

When we are "on purpose," we are on course, and adjustments are generally subtle and natural. The swings are less wide, and we feel the power of purpose, like driving the car efficiently over known terrain.

To be off course radically is to be "off purpose." It is still part of the trip, but it means we have bigger adjustments to make and lessons to learn. This is like being lost as we drive the car. Our destination becomes less visible, and our "off purpose" movements or turnings easily take us farther from center. To bring these erratic moves "on purpose," we learn our lessons and adjust course. Regardless, our purpose statement acts like a beacon to guide our way. It draws us forward, just as our desire to arrive at our destination causes us to ask directions and arrive at our destination. Similarly, to be "on purpose" can feel good, and we learn and grow by following the good feeling, as a plant grows by orienting toward the sun. Attraction draws us onward and teaches us to stay relatively "on purpose." We move toward the pleasure, developing the ability to increasingly orient toward the good feelings. In cases like this, the learning is from following the pleasure of purpose, and the moves become much less erratic.

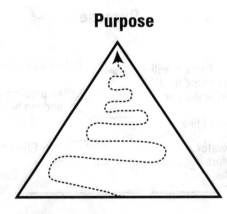

Purpose

Figure 6.5

Chad

Chad was one of five vice presidents in a civil engineering and construction firm that had risen to prominence in the early seventies on the reputation of its founder, an innovator and author. In the late eighties, the firm was still using the technologies he had developed almost twenty years earlier. Chad was the youngest senior member of the team—a strong but lone proponent of updating the firm, diversifying its consulting areas, and integrating new internal management and consulting technologies. Competition was stiffening as new technologies were introduced in engineering and information management.

Despite a shrinking bottom line, the other vice presidents consistently blocked his moves, saying too much risk was involved. Chad consistently reminded them of the company's motto: "The cutting edge of technology." They insisted they were still on the cutting edge. Chad was exasperated—he couldn't even get laptop computers for his senior consultants, who spent an enormous amount of time on planes. Finally, he decided it was no longer "on purpose" for him to continue to operate in the current structure, so he set up a contest. If his consultants sold a certain amount of business and met deadlines, he would pay for new computers out of his own bonus.

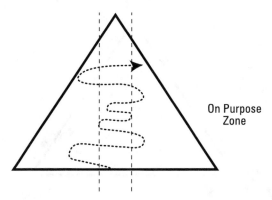

On Purpose
Zone

Figure 6.6

Senior and junior consultants alike took Chad up on his challenge. By year-end, his group had booked over a third of the company's business, and the president paid for their computers himself. Chad was beginning to make his point. He repeatedly urged the company to move into new areas, arguing that they were not yet "on purpose." The company finally allowed him to move into a new area and buy a number of software programs he needed for the venture.

By the end of the next year, his group was booking closer to fifty percent of the firm's business. He went to the owner, who was ready to retire, and told him that his personal work mission was to maximize the use of technology in helping the company's clients succeed in their ventures. It was his opinion that the firm did not agree with this, and he was going to leave if the firm did not come into line.

Today Chad is president of the company and, with his usual courage, keeps the company on course using his mission statement and purpose as the beacons to which he orients.

Chad's company had moved wide from its purpose, which kept him from his own optimal purpose fulfillment. Chad needed his company to readjust course and return to its higher purpose in order to maximize his own. In dealing with the corporation, he needed to learn more about self-assertion and being a strong team member to succeed in helping the company. It took extreme determination to turn it back on course.

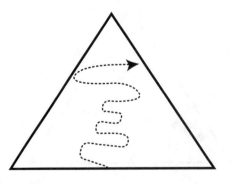

Figure 6.7

Remember that change in ourselves takes place over time and there will be times when we are slow to turn, just as Chad's company was slow to adjust. They traveled wide of their purpose line before Chad's ultimatum forced a return to center. Especially in dealing with larger companies, it is important to remember that aircraft carriers, for example, don't turn as quickly as speedboats. This doesn't mean we shouldn't adjust as soon as possible. We all saw General Motors' unnecessarily slow, incomplete turnaround when faced with Japanese and European quality, front-wheel drive, and driver/passenger-friendly environments. **(AMP)***

LEARNING FROM ADVERSITY

We learn some things from prosperity, but we learn many more from adversity . . . When things get rough, remember: it's the rubbing that brings out the shine.

...E. C. McKenzie

Despite a shrinking bottom line, Chad's company was not learning. It had strayed from its mission, as we all do. Purpose draws us forward and brings out the best in us. Adversity frequently challenges us to keep focused on purpose and at the same time teaches us some of our most purposeful lessons. It also moves us into and through problems we might otherwise have avoided.

Chad demonstrated the courage to face problems in his firm before they became catastrophic. He learned his lessons, saved the firm from extreme adversity, and forced a good deal of new corporate experimentation and learning, too. This ability to learn and adjust is critical to a life of full purpose. In the process of living true to his purpose, Chad learned how to be a better manager, developing creative solutions and becoming a

---

* AMP—Think of at least one innovation you would like to integrate into your business that would help it better fulfull its purpose.

better motivator. He grew strong as he engaged the other officers' resistance. He learned how to work in organizations more effectively and became a more focused, purposeful leader. Similarly, the firm experimented, adding and dropping programs as it forged forward with a renewed sense of purpose and zeal. Its battle is far from over, but the primary return to center has been made.

ACCEPT AND LEARN FROM FAILURE

Life is our teacher, teaching us with the good experiences and the painful ones.

...Donna Levine

Embracing adversity, especially failure, and learning from it is critical to living a purposeful life. In facing and accepting difficulties, we realize our potential.

Otto is a naturalized American, born in Poland. He had a successful career internationally in engineering and human resources for a corrugated box manufacturer but never felt he was adequately compensated for his work and travel, so he decided to use his contacts to go into the executive search business.

His search business grew more slowly than he imagined until he received an assignment from a German conglomerate to hire directors and an international team of managers to run a plant start-up in the Soviet Union. They needed directors of operations, sales, engineering, and a number of technical and staff positions to hit the ground running—a total of eleven positions. The entire contract meant $500,000 to his firm, as much as he had earned personally in the entire previous year. It turned out to be much harder to place people in the Soviet Union than he had imagined.

In order to manage the search, Otto needed researchers around the western hemisphere to locate potential candidates so he could bring the team together. The job became frustrating when people declined positions and were turned down for what he thought were peculiar reasons.

After nine months, only one hire had been made, and Otto lost the contract. He immediately blamed the Germans and his staff, deciding this was not the right kind of work for his firm. He failed to learn his lessons, because he would not accept that he had failed. He concluded that the search was impossible and that he never should have accepted it in the first place. His lessons were what we call reactive. They define him as a victim of circumstances and caused little movement toward purpose fulfillment.

Had he accepted his failure and avoided blaming others, he could have used the incident as an object lesson to strengthen and grow his firm. He would have seen that his planning skills were lacking and that his firm followed a number of inadequate procedures, especially assessment practices. By facing his lessons, Otto would have realized that the person he put in charge wasn't keeping him accurately and adequately informed. He would have seen a big blind spot in his supervision of her. He would have learned to plan better by setting deadlines and quotas, refined his candidate screening procedures, and trained or replaced his project manager. All this would have strengthened his firm and developed him further as a manager.

Top athletic teams review game films so they can learn. They tend to review losses especially closely to determine weaknesses and errors. Uncorrectable weaknesses are compensated for in future strategies, while errors and weaknesses that can be improved are dealt with in practice skill drills. Winners learn from adversity and get stronger, while losers blame, make excuses, and fall behind. **(AMP)***

---

* AMP—Identify an important business failure or setback you experienced. What did you learn from the experience? How did it help you clarify your sense of purpose? How does it help you define your current purpose statement? Identify a failure from which you have not learned. What are your blocks and "reasons"?

ACCEPTING THE TRUTH

You need to think about the true way of being a human being, not merely to be someone who has knowledge or is clever in what he does; but to be somebody who knows what he wants to do. Be one who knows that for life you require the truth.

...ALBERT SCHWEITZER

The biggest barrier to experiencing the power of purpose and living "on purpose" is failure to face the truth head on. This way, we fail to learn, grow, and fulfill our potential. Otto's major problem was his failure to accept the truth. He knew he was getting behind on the project but kept kidding himself. Had he faced this head-on, he would have realized there were problems and redoubled his efforts earlier. He might even have used the influx of capital to hire a more skilled project manager.

Equille

Equille is a courageous businessperson. In her situation, the truth was hard to swallow, but once she did, she and everyone around her came out winners. Equille was brought to Chicago from California to turn around an ailing savings and loan bank. Assessing the situation, she proudly submitted her one-, three-, and five-year plans to the parent company. Halfway through the first year, the parent company was bought out by another bank. This upset Equille, because her operation might easily have been absorbed into a division of the new company and her entire staff released. Despite her discomfort she forged on.

In the meantime, she also discovered her bank had been investing in bad situations to keep the income stream up. The loans were weak, with high default rates. Changing this policy would reduce income even further. She made the necessary moves and reduced the head count, only to discover the level of incompetence in the bank was far greater than the level represented by the original owners. It was so appalling that she had no hope of meeting the projections she had submitted to the parent company.

Rather than playing ostrich like Otto and burying her head in the sand, Equille immediately went to the parent company directors and discussed the problem. Equille reviewed the problems with them in depth, including staff strengths and weaknesses, and suggested an inventory be done of the new owner's operations to see what resources the new owner had that could help. She was courageously willing to see the branch closed or wholly absorbed. The inventory revealed complementary product mixes and skill sets in the two staffs. As a result, she and her superiors suggested several options in which the two divisions could be merged or shuffled. In one proposal, business would be passed across divisions with complementary distribution of products and clients. In another plan, Equille's entire operation would be merged into the new parent. The new owners have been impressed by Equille's integrity and courage and, most recently, she has been appointed as the new managing director of the joint operation.

As of this writing, the transactions are still open, but whichever way they go, Equille can look at herself in the mirror and be satisfied—she faced difficult facts and lived true to her purpose, which required the best service to depositors, investors, employees, and owners. Because Equille accepted the truth, she was able to propose open, creative, and purposeful actions, creating a win for all involved.

MOVE THROUGH BLOCKS

We must never despair; our situation has been compromising before, and it has changed for the better; so I trust it will again. If new difficulties arise, we must put forth new exertion.

...George Washington

We all get stuck in life. Blocks are barriers that stop us from moving ahead. Purpose helps us move through barriers we face and requires that we face barriers head on. When we move through blocks we reorient to the on-purpose line, learn lessons, and move forward. Salesmen must face barriers like call reluctance, managers must tell people things they do not want to hear—we all have projects we avoid and other moves we fail to make. Any impediment to our forward movement is a block.

Blocks happen more than we might consider. We make a call we fear and someone is not there so we want to quit, a team member does not do what we expect, information is harder to come by than we anticipate, and on and on. How often have we become immobilized or slowed, complaining rather than moving through the block?

When we hold our purpose before us, it helps give us the impetus to address our blocks and move on. Frequently, owners of businesses sense urgency in problems and move through them more quickly than employees, who lack the same perspective. Purpose can help provide that urgency.

Blocks seem to occur in cycles, just as work tends to be accomplished in cycles of high activity alternating with periods of relatively lower activity. We all have times of high productivity and periods of slower movement, no matter how hard we try. Purpose helps us maximize the high-productivity periods and minimize the less productive times. Moving through blocks is key to keeping on purpose.

LARGE BLOCKS

Doris was in her sixth year at the consulting firm where she sold and delivered strategic planning services, only one of the many product lines offered by her company. Her career had been all right but nothing she was especially proud of. In her last review, the partners told her that her present performance did not warrant a partnership position. Her projects were always the same, and she did not seem to be growing. Her sales were erratic, and her coworkers were frustrated with her. She had developed a reputation internally for unresponsiveness, and it was a common joke around the firm that she treated e-mail messages like a fine wine, leaving them on the shelf to age. This and other revelations shocked her into a new sense of urgency. Partner selections began at year eight, and if she hadn't made partner by year ten, she would be asked to leave.

She began selling more business and did fine for about three months, but her performance fell back to her previous levels. No matter how hard she tried, she just couldn't seem to keep going consistently. Seeing the problem recurring, she sought coaching from the senior partner in charge of her area. The partner began by helping Doris define her purpose and mission. Doris was shocked to discover how little she had focused on her mission, which was to support her clients' success. Making the sale was as far as she could see. When she began heeding her mission and digging deeper into her clients' problems, sales started happening naturally as a result of service. Not only was she selling more, she was beginning to bring in more interesting, complex jobs.

One of her key clients began having trouble, so the client brought Doris in to help. She became intensely involved but felt inadequate, so she overcame her fear of appearing incompetent and began bringing senior partners in on the job. This was scary for her, since she feared losing respect in the client's eyes. Just the opposite happened—they began bringing more problems to her attention! She learned and grew as she helped. She read related articles like never before to find ways to help her client. Her skill base was expanding rapidly, and her stock with partners and the client soared.

Without noticing it, she had begun consistently billing more hours than ever before. She developed a real sense of mission and began caring deeply about other clients too. Her team skills were expanding as she improved coworker relations, too. Bringing in more and more colleagues in different practice areas, she found her service expanding exponentially. She not only helped clients develop more in-depth strategic plans but also stayed around now to be sure they were implemented. She clarified her service mission as helping her clients succeed in their own missions to the best of her ability.

Her mission statement carried her through downturns in her sales activity and caused her to burn through blocks in projects. Her image in the firm changed from that of leech to "net giver." She billed big hours and bagged bigger projects. She believed in what she was doing for the first time in her career.

Although she was significantly busier, her e-mail messages were tended to better, and she made more calls to potential clients than ever. Her secretary found her planning improved, and she delegated to younger consultant/trainers more effectively. She became known as a top staff developer. Problems that would have stopped her in the past were insignificant blips on her screen as she managed the largest project in the company's history. Her partnership election is pending, but her recent reviews have all been superior. Whether she makes partner or not this time around, she feels good about herself. She's a woman with a mission who moves through blocks where she used to pull up a chaise lounge to rest. **(AMP)***

NO EXCUSES

The man who really wants to do something finds a way; the other man finds an excuse.

...E. C. McKenzie

Excuses inhibit purposeful living. They cut us off from deeper truths. It's important that we look below the surface. One of the greatest barriers to overcoming our blocks and fulfilling our purpose is excuses that keep our understanding superficial. Excuses keep us from fully and accurately assessing where we are. Without really knowing where we are, we are less likely to get where we are going.

It's like asking directions to New York and, when asked where we are coming from, saying Chicago instead of New Orleans. The directions simply won't help. Similarly, not accurately assessing our situation because of excuses keeps us from knowing where we are, so we can't get directly where we are go-

---

* AMP—Identify a time where having a clear sense of purpose or mission helped you move through difficulties more easily. Could you have put your purpose into words at that time? Could you now? Do you find it helpful to consciously define your purpose, as opposed to leaving it more vague and intuitive? Why?

ing. This causes inefficiencies at best. Looking beneath the surface, refusing our own excuses gives us valuable information necessary to our success. We saw this problem in Otto. He made excuses for his problems, which were always someone else's fault. Doris's career never "took off' until she quit her excuses and began facing accurately where the problems came from. Avoiding excuses keeps us from the truth and good problem-solving. Excuses ultimately keep us from our purpose and really knowing ourselves.

KNOW YOURSELF

> *To get into the core of God at his greatest, one must first get into the core of himself at his least.*
>
> ...JOHANNES ECKHARDT

Self-knowledge is a lifelong process. Self-knowledge gives us more accurate analysis, more effective problem-solving, better planning, team building, management, etc. We just saw how Doris's journey began with her discovery that she was not on a partnership pace. Accepting this began her journey of self-acceptance and self-knowledge. Each step of her journey led her deeper into awareness of her clients' needs and her own limitations. Once she faced her shortcomings and brought in senior consultants, she could relax and learn. She delighted in her strengths and was challenged by her weaknesses. The more she moved into new consulting territory, the more she learned about her clients and herself. Each new skill she undertook revealed unknown strengths, weaknesses, attitudes, barriers, and capacities.

The door to self-knowledge does not open all at one once. We forget what we once knew, and we have significant areas of awareness to develop. The door must be opened over and over again. In some ways the opening gets easier, and in some ways it becomes harder, but fulfilling our highest purpose is tightly aligned with learning and growing. The greatest challenge is learning about and developing ourselves. To know ourselves, we must master our minds. Mind mastery is key to full self-development and purpose fulfillment.

MIND MASTERY

One man who has a mind and knows it can always beat ten men who haven't and don't.

...GEORGE BERNARD SHAW

Discipline does not mean suppression and control, nor is it adjustment to a pattern or ideology. It means the mind sees 'what is' and learns from 'what is.'

...JIDDU KRISHNA MURTI

My favorite example of mastery of the mind is the story of Jacques Lusseyran, as told in his autobiography, *And There Was Light*. Lusseyran was, at sixteen, the founding publisher and editor of what was to become *France Soire*, the most important daily newspaper in Paris.*

Lusseyran lived in Paris under the suffocating control of German occupation in World War II. He organized the powerful underground resistance organization called the Volunteers of Liberty, which kept German-occupied Paris informed about the outside world. Managing the activities of over six hundred boys and young men, he kept all the details of their movement and over one thousand telephone numbers, safe and free from German discovery—in his head. His resistance work was a demanding, full-time job. He planned schedules, edited papers, coordinated deliveries, and trained his workers to avoid capture by the occupation forces. Simultaneously, he managed to attend thirty hours of school classes per week and studied another

---

* Jacques Lusseyran. *And There Was Light* (New York: Parabola Press, 1987).

thirty hours to graduate in the top one percent of his high school and university classes, in what the French call the upper first.

Lusseyran was captured and sent to the Buchenwald death camp, where he would have been killed if he hadn't convinced the Germans he spoke Russian—which he didn't, but learned as he went. In Buchenwald he was a leader in inmate life, helping with healing and maintaining contact with the outside. He survived severe brushes with death and was ultimately responsible for a good part of the only lives saved in Buchenwald, where a reported eighty thousand were machine-gunned to death even as Patton's Third Army was racing to save them.

His is a most remarkable story, all the more so considering it had all happened by the time Lusseyran was twenty years old—not to mention that he was totally blind from the age of eight! Living through Buchenwald alone was miraculous, since it is commonly thought that invalids were exterminated upon entry.

Lusseyran had to learn mind mastery early in his life. If he hadn't, he would have lived a very limited life or died many different times. He needed to master his mind in order to get around in a sighted world—it was necessary for him to fulfill his purpose, which he saw as performing the will of God. He learned to perceive details that his sighted friends would miss as he ran through the mountains with a hand on their shoulder. He tapped energy most of us would never even dream exists. All of this was possible only through powerful purpose and mastery of his mental functions. This mastery gave him strength and powers beyond what most of us would even dream to yearn for:

> The well of my strength never dried up. The later I stayed up, the better I slept. The more I learned, the more I was able to learn. My memory only knew how to say yes. It made room for everything, from the thousand and fifty Paris telephone numbers I needed for my work in the Resistance . . . (which I had learned by heart in 1942 to keep from writing anything down). It made room for the system of monads according to Leibnitz, for Turkish history in the nineteenth century, even for those fifteen pages from the letters of Cicero in Latin. . . .

My mind was a world in growth, one which had not found its limits. . . .

I had not yet acquired the hardness of a man and was still as resilient as a child, a fact which accounts for my accomplishments between 1941 and 1943. When I think of them now at the mid-point of life with its weariness, I find it hard to understand them.

Lusseyran was living a life of heightened purpose, which helps explain some of his accomplishments, as do his great natural gifts and a profound faith in the Creator that he heavily relied upon.

From early on he engaged in mastering his mind. Thanks to his parents' positive attitude, he avoided considering himself a victim. "Grown-up people forget that children never complain against circumstances—unless, of course, grown-ups are so foolish as to suggest it to them. For an eight-year-old, what is is always best." Lusseyran saw himself as creator of his own reality. Most of all, he lived true to his purpose and the higher principles that went along with it. "That is what you had to do to live in the camp [Buchenwald]: be engaged, not live for yourself alone. The self-centered life has no place. . . . You must go beyond it, lay hold of something outside of yourself."

Mastery of the mind required allowing himself no denial. He had to fearlessly accept the truth, accept real limitations and refuse imagined ones. Likewise, he could not afford excuses like minimization or rationalization. He needed to be deeply in contact with reality at all times. He overcame apparently insurmountable barriers. Blame was exiled. It would reduce his power and ability to influence his world, for which he needed his full capacities.

He developed an ability to perceive the world around him that surpassed, in many ways, his sighted friends' abilities. His "sight" depended on mastery of his mind, "I could no longer afford to be jealous or unfriendly because, as soon as I was, a bandage came down over my eyes and I was bound, hand and foot, and cast aside. . . . fear . . . anger and impatience had the same effect, throwing everything into confusion." Mastering his mind kept him open to the universe of possibilities. It helped him live "on purpose."

Mind mastery is a lifelong pursuit. It is necessary for the fullest living of purpose. Until we attain full purpose mastery, following the principles of purpose helps keep us "on course."

Living our purpose fully requires high skill levels in many more areas than we can cover here. For most of us, the power of purpose can be tapped most fully when we use intermediary, more accessible tools to live to our highest.

In waterskiing, the best skiers can ski barefoot. For the rest of us, skis help a lot. The principles of purpose are like the skiis. They help us as we learn to live in the full power of absolute focus on purpose. The principles of purpose keep us on course when we can't see even our purpose clearly, just as a compass orients a sailor when the sun and stars are lost in cloud cover. Let's now consider these principles in detail.

Chapter 7

Winning with the Principles of Personal Purpose

It is often easier to fight for principles than to live up to them.
...ADLAI STEVENSON

In theory, each moment of our lives would be measured and guided by purpose. In fact, purpose is a rarefied abstraction, and few of us have the skill and awareness to live this way. Even if we could live in almost perfect consciousness, most of us couldn't be sure which of many alternatives life presents to us is the most "on purpose." Because we are still developing, we have many lessons to learn that will only be understood as we vary from the centerline to the extreme and learn. To know which act is "on purpose" requires a high level of skill. When I first introduced the company purpose to our staff in 1981, they thought it was nice but useless. It took the quickest members two years to use the abstraction powerfully.

Until we are capable of daily, momentary navigation by purpose and until transcendental principles like love and compassion guide all we do, we will do well to use the less abstract, more accessible principles of purpose to guide our daily lives. One common element to most of our ultimate life purposes is the full development of self to our highest most mature functioning in the world. The principles of purpose universally enhance our development personally, professionally, and spiritually. They are like rungs of a ladder to higher purpose and consciousness.

Each principle can be used as a guideline to living a life of purpose. Principles of purpose give us a more immediate, available, instructive, and effective way to act purposefully. We can increase our sense of purpose by learning to live by the principles of purpose moment by moment. The principles of purpose give us a way to transcend our limitations, helping us scale the heights of our greatest potential. By focusing on them, we naturally move into new creative territory like an adventurer, following the trail indicated by the principles.

These are principles common to all people. Artists, businessmen, engineers, housewives, and students can all fulfill their life purpose by living in consonance with them.

These principles are normal parts of human development. They define key stages in our growth, leading naturally toward a life of higher purpose. Following them gives us the fullest satisfaction, engagement, and development. These principles were integral to our purpose in childhood and remain so today. Consciously applying them as adults contributes to completion of

Figure 7.1

unfinished business, learning of daily lessons, and an expanding sense of mature purpose. Just as athletes return to basics to exit slumps and return to peak performance, we return to the foundational principles of purpose fulfillment.

The first principle of purpose, **aliveness**, is the basic principle upon which the rest are based. It is primarily operant in the newborn to six months of age. **Play** comes next, primary in the infant up to three years of age. **Intention** is key to the toddler from the terrible twos into pubescence. **Expression** of truth to our highest vision is the challenge to the adolescent, while **commitment** guides and provides challenge to the young adult. Finally, **responsibility** must be mastered by the mature adult for ultimate purpose fulfillment.

In this chapter, we will see how the principles of personal purpose, aliveness, play, intention, truth to our highest vision, commitment, and responsibility build on each other and are necessary for a fulfilling life of personal purpose.

ALIVENESS

Purpose without aliveness is like a boat without water; it loses meaning and function.

The more alive we live, the more purposeful our behavior. Work without aliveness is dull. If we are not animated, meetings are torturous and our days seem like never-ending prison sentences. Aliveness in the workplace means animated, high-energy, vital production and fulfilling, successful interaction. At work, aliveness means more engagement and quicker turnarounds. With aliveness, work is more fun, and we are more effective and less controlled.

Aliveness is the primary animating principle, the foundation for all other principles of purpose. Without aliveness, life itself would not exist. It is the primary principle in the newborn. Parents protect with all their being to assure life.

Each principle has a polarity. The opposite of aliveness is deadness, or the absence of life. Deadness at work means a slow day, victimhood, and joyless effort. Fear is the emotion that causes us to dampen our aliveness and become dead. Parents who let fear dictate their behavior become overprotective and limit their child's aliveness.

Throughout our workday, we choose between aliveness and deadness. Choice is the principle by which we create our lives moment by moment. Author Viktor Frankl examined attitudes of people who survived concentration camps. He showed us that even in these brutal inhuman environments we have choice. We can, at the very least, choose our attitude and reactions to the worst of circumstances. We saw this in the story of Jacques Lusseyran in Buchenwald.

Too often we choose deadness in our daily business life. Just look at how many meetings throughout the business world are full of participants sitting around conference tables, bored, angry, or afraid, withholding their true thoughts. Why? They're afraid they'll be rejected, attacked, or even lose their jobs if they are not careful. Repressing our aliveness may be necessary on occasion, but when it becomes a chronic condition or lifestyle we deaden ourselves, limiting our purpose and reducing our effectiveness.

Each of us, in some individual way, chooses deadness over aliveness. To the extent we do this, we leave room to develop our purpose further. As we grow in our purpose, we grow in aliveness and the full expression of the other principles. Similarly, living with full aliveness enhances purpose fulfillment.

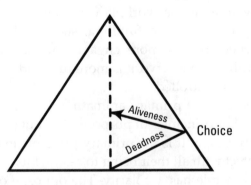

Figure 7.2

Live Life Fully—Tony

Life is not lost in dying; life is lost minute by minute, day by dragging day, in all the thousand uncaring ways (we go about it).

...Stephen Vincent Benet

Tony is a first-generation Italian-American who grew up in an expressive and animated home. Years ago, when our story begins, he was the accountant in charge of receivables for a hospital. Earlier in his career, Tony had been told by several of his supervisors and coworkers that he had to stop waving his hands around and talking so much if he expected anyone to take him seriously. He took this coaching to heart and stifled himself at work. Unfortunately, he also became more reserved at home. He progressed well in his career but failed to experience the fulfillment he expected.

At a seminar on career development, Tony learned about life purpose and the principle of aliveness. He began rethinking his position, knowing his wife was unhappy with his distance created by his deadness and that he had been finding his work more and more drudgery. He started by addressing his barriers to being fully alive and discovered that fear of rejection was primary. He had been unconsciously shutting down. He committed to keeping himself fully alive at work and at home. Asking himself what full aliveness would mean in meetings, he developed a picture of himself saying what he really thought and joking with the staff, including the owner—expressing his disagreements with some of the company's ways of operating.

Tony has a wicked, irreverent sense of humor, and his coworkers were taken aback when he first began expressing it. This scared Tony, too, but he noticed that nothing terrible happened—a few people even started responding playfully, including the owner.

Expressing his disagreement with the company policy of ninety-day payments was the real test for Tony. He knew that his boss, the comptroller, and the owner both figured the extra three months' interest meant a good deal of passive income for the institution. Checks were written on time, but they were placed in "to be mailed" boxes for ninety days. Vendors who complained repeatedly might receive a check early, but they had to make a lot of noise to get it. Tony began by running his concerns by coworkers, who all agreed. They were embarrassed daily as they fielded vendor calls and felt ashamed talking to the ones who just kept quiet and patiently waited.

The tension in the room was as thick as cold taffy the day Tony suggested changes in the unofficial payment policy to the comptroller and owner. He reasoned that the hospital wanted everyone else to pay on time, so turnabout seemed fair play—a way of doing unto others as the hospital would have others do unto it. Simply speaking about the problem broke numerous organizational taboos and rules. An awkward silence followed Tony's presentation. The comptroller pointed out that Tony was young and idealistic and did not understand the demands of the "real world." Tony held his ground, asking what was so unreal about his suggestion. What if he were to tell all the patients and insurance companies they had ninety days to pay? Now that would be unreal! The comptroller defended the policy, saying the insurance companies did pay late. Things really began to heat up.

The president stopped the conversation after a while, but in the future, at every opportunity, Tony went on discussing this and other issues with which he took exception. His persistence was difficult. It required vigilance to not allow his fear and desire to be liked to cause him to desist. Stopping his expression would have equated to deadness for him. He kept up the campaign. Sometimes he won, but most times he lost. Even so, he was learning to express his aliveness and overcoming his fear. He liked and respected himself better this way, even if it meant being fired or not being promoted as he wished. Today he is comptroller and was recently considered for the position of director, to replace the retiring owner.

By expressing his aliveness, Tony began contributing more to his company, furthering his and the institution's purpose. Had he been in a less tolerant environment, Tony might have been fired. Although this might have seemed disastrous, being released because of our commitment to higher purpose can represent an opportunity to align at a higher level with an environment where we are more likely to be appreciated and have institutional support for our higher purpose.

Aliveness can be expressive or receptive. Riotous laughter, full-blown rage, heated passion—as well as holding hands, watching a sunset, and meditating in blissful peace—can all be expressions of aliveness. In Tony's case, aliveness came through expression, but we're just as likely to find people who need to contain their expression and learn to be more receptive in order to become more alive and purposeful.

Suppressing our aliveness is normal in the world the way it is. When we were young, as infants, our aliveness was limited and channeled as we were socialized. As adults, we face the challenge of reclaiming this repressed aliveness, unleashing and harnessing it to carry us fully forward to accomplish our higher purposes. Each of the first three principles has an emotion we must deal with successfully to live it fully. We must overcome unrealistic and realistic fears to experience full aliveness. We saw Tony do this, overcoming his fear of rejection and firing.

Heroes like Joan of Arc, George Washington, Martin Luther King, and Gandhi faced fear and experienced full aliveness and immediacy of their purpose. In the same way, Tony faced his fear and he unleashed his aliveness. Overcoming fear, where appropriate, vaults us over the hurdle. Fear is, in fact, repressed aliveness—a useful emotion when it warns us of true danger but problematic when it keeps us from moving forward with our higher purpose.

Many corporations resist aliveness. Too often, companies instill fear to keep people in line and avoid errors. In addition, individuals in even the most open, forgiving, accepting environments are very often afraid because of personal history and as a result, fail to thrive fully. Put organizational intolerance and personal fear together and we see too many employees whose careers are focused on avoiding mistakes rather than expressing life fully and fulfilling their own and their companies' higher purposes.

The challenge of being fully alive and reclaiming our re-pressed aliveness extends throughout our lives, just as the call to purposeful living extends continually before us. By keeping our purpose in our sights, we increase our experience of aliveness. By living toward more and more aliveness, we automatically enhance our purposeful living.

Anywhere at work—in meetings or on the shop floor—we can ask ourselves if we are being fully alive. We can then choose new ways of doing and being that reduce deadness and increase our aliveness or animation. We can remind ourselves to choose more alive alternatives and move more "on purpose." **(AMP)***

PLAY

Make your work play and your play work.
        …PHIL JACKSON

Work is play for pay in this model. Playful work is engaging work. It is challenging and causes us to develop. It is not necessarily amusing. Play is aliveness in relationship. It is a here-and-now interaction between me and something or someone (or even myself) that results in nourishment and growth. In early childhood, play is the principle that predominates as we develop a sense of identity. Play is the principle of interaction—it is through interaction that we are reflected back to ourselves. In this way, we are defined by our world and come to know our-

---

* AMP 1—Define aliveness for yourself. Give examples of things you do to express your aliveness.

* AMP 2—What risks would you like to take to be more alive at work? In other areas of your life?

* AMP 3—Is there one new step you would like to take now to be more alive? What would it be?

* AMP 4—What fears keep you from expressing your aliveness? (If you can't think of any, you are probably out of touch. Fear is a normal, necessary part of human experience.) List three situations where you find yourself holding back your aliveness in your life.

selves. Play comes to focus in the infant of six months to three years old. Interacting and being reflected are necessary for the development of self-esteem. The more consistently and accurately positive the feedback we receive, the higher the self-esteem we develop.

We've all experienced play firsthand—when our work was acknowledged, we had a warm interaction, or a project went satisfyingly well. These positive experiences enhance our self-esteem and act as encouragement to keep us expanding into our world rather than just getting by. When this happens enough, we develop sufficient self-esteem to face failure and hard times, as did Thomas Edison and Abraham Lincoln.

Play happens in the here and now, since it is only in the here and now we can experience contact. We've all experienced the hunger for affirmation that play satisfies. We experience hurt when we are not acknowledged and affirmed. We know it also when we are negatively reflected in the case of disapproval by someone whose opinion matters to us. Is it any wonder that work can be unsatisfying for so many when either this hunger is denied or no affirmation from the environment is forthcoming?

At work, play manifests in innumerable ways: discussion, cooperation, satisfaction, teamwork, and, ultimately, success. In play, information is exchanged more freely, and we feel more fulfilled. Work feels more exciting and engaging. We learn and grow—our teams function better and better. Camaraderie and interaction increase. We may make more mistakes or even have more conflict, but the quality of our experience is increased and we learn and grow from better nourishment.

Burden is the polarity of play. Throughout our lives, we choose between the nourishment of play and the starvation of burden. Without a sense of play at work, we experience burden. Our time is heavy; we seem to atrophy rather than grow. High level, here-and-now, nourishing interaction in the workplace means high-energy, cooperative work teams, people who want to be doing exactly what they are doing—with excitement, mutuality, and engagement. Following is the story of one who learned to play by remembering to interact and to do it fully.

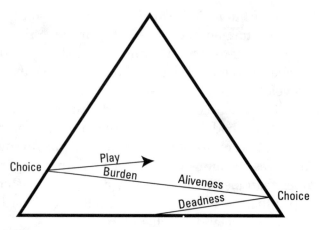

Figure 7.3

Interact Fully for Nourishment and Growth—Raisha

Raisha is a pediatrician. Not only was she board certified and widely published, she was in high demand as a keynote speaker for professional and parent groups. Her career as a top researcher at a widely recognized teaching institution meant she was able to engage in all the activities she said she wanted. She got to speak and lecture around the world, see patients, do research, publish, and lead grand rounds.

Despite all this, her career began to seem routine to her, and she came in to see me to discuss what was next. Conversation revealed that she was not fulfilled because she kept aloof. She didn't feel she had time for what she called the "mundanities" of hospital and university life. Furthermore, she was not integrated into the hospital unit, because she had no administrative responsibility.

Upon examination, it occurred to Raisha that an element was missing in her career and purpose, so she finally responded to one of the many job offers she received from other hospitals. This situation was ideal. Raisha could keep her position teaching and researching at her current university hospital and become chief of service and start a pediatric program, including outpatient and inpatient services, at a newly restructured, smaller suburban hospital.

Raisha was determined to make this situation more challenging and fulfilling. She decided to focus on greater fulfillment by forcing herself to engage in more interaction. She felt that alone, her ability to play was significant. Her research and general performance showed this, but in the face of others, like staff with problems for her to solve, she had always withdrawn, and she felt dragged down. She had kept to herself—surprisingly, despite her wide range of professional acknowledgment and responsibility—treating fellow staff as a burden.

The administrative challenge of the new unit seemed just the ticket for her to expand her skills. She accepted the position in June and spent the next two months planning the August opening of her unit. She became aware of both excitement and fear about her new venture. She began planning how she wanted to be as a leader—immediate, accessible, and involved. In other words, she wanted to play fully. This would prove to be quite a stretch from her forte in studies, research, and debate.

August arrived, and Raisha went to her first staff meeting determined to enroll the team in a mutual, engaging, challenging voyage together. She surprised herself when she opened by telling them how much this meant to her and how scared of failure she was. Her immediate vulnerability was compelling to them, dispelling her image as the distant star and making her "their star." She completed her first week excited at the range of interactions she had had and returning each day hungry for more.

Her staff flourished, and Raisha's unit became known as a place where staff grew in both technical and humanitarian ways. Her people moved on to direct other services. Patients flocked to them at a time when other hospitals were desperately seeking business. The unit's community mission led it to start numerous parent support groups and educational programs. Raisha's renown brought important resources to the community. Her staff was proud to be of service.

Raisha had learned the fulfillment of here-and-now interaction. She had learned to choose play more often than burden in dealing with individuals and the institution. She was routinely nourished and grew, from both the easy and difficult aspects of the job. She learned to reach out in hard times and consistently found the support and affirmation she needed to face challenges of all orders.

When we play, not only are we less lonely, the contact with others affirms us and actually helps us grow. We develop our capacities fully. In Raisha's case, we see how her contagious, playful purpose caused her staff to develop and her community to benefit. **(AMP)***

Raisha's life purpose was being nicely fulfilled as she focused on one principle. This is a useful strategy, to focus on one principle at a time. Progress in living any of the principles translates directly to increased purpose fulfillment. Raisha was a quick study—as was Courtney, who found a good business playmate to help her learn and grow fast.

PLAY ENHANCES RAPPORT

Courtney heads a design and publishing support firm with her husband. She is the head writer, and her husband heads graphic design. For Courtney, sales was always a tough challenge, coming up with the best proposal and winning contracts over competition she rarely knew. She felt driven to compete with these unknown enemies. Sales was, consequently, an adversarial challenge of convincing and winning. She had no frame of reference for sales to be a cooperative, nourishing activity. Courtney dis-

---

* AMP 1—How much of your work would you describe as play? How much is burden?

* AMP 2—What are the factors that make your work playful? How important are relationships with others to the sense of play?

* AMP 3—Think of some ways you can choose to play more at home and at work.

covered the value of play and mutuality with clients in just such a tense, highly competitive situation.

Courtney's client was the head of benefits consulting for a major national consulting firm. His firm had just been acquired by a much larger firm. Her client, Stan, was a freethinker. He wanted Courtney to bid on a major redesign project that would take up to two years and require dealing with the purchasing firm's benefits people and design staff.

Stan assured Courtney ahead of time that management of the design process was going to be more important than specific ideas. Stan's view was that the project would evolve over time. This approach was upsetting to Courtney, who was used to winning projects on the strength of her designs and executing a specific plan.

Courtney took Stan's lead and decided to go into the next meeting with the parent company staff with play in mind, intent on developing rapport and discussion rather than making a good definitive presentation. This was a completely new approach, and she was apprehensive.

The meeting went great, to Courtney's relief. However, the project kept getting put off. Courtney went to visit Stan and expressed her concern. She had decided to play fully and engage in relationship with Stan rather than wait for the verdict from on high, as she had always done in the past. She asked questions about the organization and began diagnosing the problems with Stan. He told her things about the company and its politics that really opened her eyes about decision making in his and other corporations. She was already growing in understanding and sales ability by leaps and bounds in just one playful sales encounter. Courtney discovered that contrary to what she had suspected, the delay had nothing to do with the acquisition or the new parent company.

As she and Stan talked long and hard about the company and the forces at play in the decision, she discovered that the marketing department did not like the fact that Stan was heading a project of this magnitude outside their department and, furthermore, already had a "pet" design firm it had used for ten years. The head of the design firm was a golfing buddy with the president of Stan's parent company. Stan had to satisfy his own marketing department to get Courtney in on such a big project. Rather than an open bidding situation, this was a case of Stan trying to create an opening. They discussed various strategies together.

Courtney found this level of partnership adventurous and rewarding. She was further surprised when Stan said, "I don't know why I'm telling you all this. I don't speak this frankly with anyone, in or outside the firm." She began making routine visits to Stan, just to chat. Sales was becoming a matter of relationship, and a game she enjoyed. Courtney's ability to play deepened her rapport with Stan, and he partnered with her at a level that was fulfilling and growth promoting for both of them. Problem solving and repeated stabs at the situation helped Stan evolve a plan that allowed marketing to have its firm oversee the project as long as Courtney's firm did the writing. **(AMP)***

Courtney refused to submit to her sense of burden and defeat and kept going in the face of problems beyond what she could previously have imagined. The whole adventure was a big step ahead for Courtney but typical of the fulfillment and growth available when we engage fully in the here and now and play in business. To be sure, we'll have defeats, but we'll win more, too, and have the ultimate victory of fulfilling our purpose by developing ourselves as fully as possible in nourishment and fulfillment.

---

* AMP 1—How would you describe your level of rapport with: boss(es); colleagues; reports; clients/customers?

* AMP 2—How can you choose to play more with each?

INTENTION

It is an individual's deeds, his acts which reveal his true intentions — no matter what he says.

...THOMAS BEAMES

Not only did Courtney learn to play in order to engage more fully in her sales work, she developed a strong ability of positive intention with her staff. Her strong positive intention caused her to stay engaged until she attained the results she found acceptable. This was totally new, since she had regularly felt thwarted by her teams in the past. She played harder, and they came along. Her play had become more directional and developed into creative intention. They began meeting deadlines, communicated more clearly, and felt as if they had all moved into a higher gear—accomplishing more with less effort and greater fulfillment. Intention is the driver of purpose from our survival needs on up to our highest urges to love and creation.

Intention is aliveness in direction or desire. It is through intention that we create our world. We hear most often and see intention perhaps most clearly in the developing child of around age two—the terrible twos, when the child wants what it wants with total investment. With intention, we first define ourselves by what we resist (like the two-year old saying "no") and then increasingly assert our will in positive directions toward our desires. In developing positive intention and assertion, we develop a sense that our lives are our own, not something that just happened to us.

For the two-year-old, possessing interesting objects in the grocery store takes on life-and-death importance. The once delightful child becomes impossible, resisting its mother's will with a mighty "NO!" or "Mine!" that would shake the adult workplace.

The polarity of intent is victimhood. In victimhood, we give up on direct, powerful, effective expression of our desires and choose unconsciously or intend to be acted upon by a world that controls us and our fate. In work, victimhood leads to depressed environments, poor problem-solving, blame, and many levels of hostility, from repressed to overt. In victimhood, we abdicate the power of direct intention and actually intend victimhood.

WANT FULLY

Sooner murder an infant in its cradle than nurse unacted desires.
...WILLIAM BLAKE

Imagine if we could harness the power of the willful two-year old for our positive purposes! That's just what we are suggesting here—that asserting our will fully is key to fulfilling our purpose. Few of us made the developmental leap to asserting our will fully. To some extent we have all chosen some amount of victimhood. We need to learn to give ourselves totally to experience our lives consciously as an extension of our will if we are ever to live lives of full purpose. To give ourselves fully we must first master our intention—the form of wanting that leads us toward our highest, most purposeful yearnings. Purpose re-

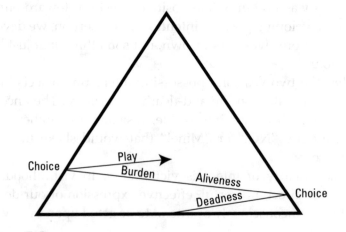

Figure 7.4

flects our highest ideal and most essential wants. By learning to assert our will, we expand our capacity to fulfill our purpose. By wanting fully, we learn to follow our heart. Our lives become a reflection of our deepest desires rather than our darkest fears.

This does not mean squashing others, which would rarely be "on purpose." It also does not mean always getting our way. It means being able to concentrate on our intended outcomes, to persist in the face of failure, to make our lives deeply our own. Too often in business, the intention of the boss or company precludes the intention of the employee. It is difficult and requires significant skill to have a mutual relationship in that situation, just as a parent finds it difficult to relate to and not to crush the child's will, when it goes against plans.

Mutually aligned intentions mean highly unified, top-producing work teams. Here, we truly get the best out of each member, because the product reflects each person's highest, fullest intention.

In graduate school, I wanted two advanced clinic experiences—none of the first-year options appealed to me. My intention to have both was strong. The second-year positions were three days a week; the first year, only two. If I were accepted, the clinic would accept me for two days as a first year student and lose a day of service. The director of one of the programs turned me down four times. I saw no other way to get the training I wanted. I repeatedly stopped by, phoned, and sent notes, until he finally exclaimed in exasperation, "You just won't take no for an answer, will you?" Of course, I said, "No." My persistence paid off, and my time there was one of the richest training experiences in my life, working with top flight, renowned clinicians in a wide array of disciplines.

Persistence and perseverance are the hallmarks of positive intention. Many of us have heard the story of Thomas Edison and the many failures he endured before succeeding in creating the first incandescent light. His attitude was important here; when asked if he was getting discouraged, he responded "no," that he had found lots of ways not to make a light bulb. He had harnessed the intention of the two-year-old and tempered it with maturity, endurance, and focus for the ultimate service of humanity and the ultimate fulfillment of his life purpose.

Intention is the force behind most of the great breakthroughs in human history. John Paul Jones showed absolute intention, beating the British from a sinking ship. Rosa Parks's intentions and strength heralded the civil rights movement, and Martin Luther King showed great intention in standing firm for both change and nonviolent action.

The same heroism and bravery can be seen in mothers and fathers doing their best at home and work, in salespeople who make astounding goals, in researchers who strive to find elegant solutions for "unsolvable" problems, and in less gifted persons who succeed despite their limitations.

The polarity of intention, victimhood, is accompanied by guilt and shame. We become victims because we experienced shame and broken will to some extent early on. When our will is broken, we lose the sense of being in charge of our lives and begin blaming ourselves and others for our failures. We give up living the lives we want and severely diminish our ability to live purposefully. Even the greatest captains of industry I have met exhibit some victimhood at times, complaining of employees, competition, or their wives with victimhood. We must monitor and master our victimhood and shame, countering with positive intention in order to live fully to our highest purpose. **(AMP)***

DEALING WITH ANGER: INTENDING OUR HIGHEST

> *Alderians view anger not as an overwhelming governor of behavior but as one of the emotions which the individual creates to move him toward his goal.*
>
> ...THOMAS BEAMES

---

* AMP—Recall an example when you used persistence and perseverance to fulfill an important intention. Did this also help you live more purposefully? How?

Many of us break down in the development of strong creative intention, becoming angry or giving up. Anger eats away at us, and despair causes deep unconscious resentment.

Applying our intent requires integrating and transforming the energy in anger into direct, creative action. Rather than turning in on itself, the anger impels us toward our goal. At its roots, anger is pure intent. When you think about it, anger stems from one of two experiences—pain and the desire to rid ourselves of a hurt, or pleasure and the desire to attain a pleasurable object or experience. So the unconscious positive intent of anger is always either to enhance pleasure or reduce pain.

Tom, a friend of mine, tested for an advanced black belt in a martial art. For the first test, his instructor sent a single challenger, whom Tom dispatched with ease. Next was an assailant with a weapon. Over and over, increasing numbers of unarmed assailants were followed by armed ones. Tom was growing fatigued but was careful throughout to maintain impeccable form. The onslaught continued. Tom had never dealt with more than three assailants in any previous test. After fending off four armed attackers, Tom's arms and legs were like lead. He remained confident in his form, however, and felt sure the test was over.

To his dismay, he was assaulted by five unarmed attackers, and in his weariness, began making mistakes and barely dispatched them. He prayed that the test was over, but five armed men appeared. Tom sank into an instant of victimhood and despair before experiencing something he could only describe by saying, "I snapped." He became enraged at his instructors and attackers. Power he'd never before experienced flowed through his limbs. He forgot all his careful attention to form and dispatched the group as easily as he had the first attacker.

The test was over. It had had nothing to do with form, as Tom had imagined. He had already proven expertise in form. Instead, his instructors wanted to see if he could master and integrate his rage. From our perspective, Tom passed the test, mastering his anger and transforming it into greater positive intent. It worked for, not against him.

This does not mean, however, that anger is necessary to intent. To the contrary, intent transcends anger. When we are dominated by our indulgence in or avoidance of anger, we limit the availability of our intent for our positive purposes. Courtney mastered her intent as she focused on rapport with Stan and salvaged work out of a nearly impossible situation. Gandhi showed great intent, and Lusseyran showed play and mastery of intent in overcoming the limitations of blindness and the German army. If he lost control in anger, he was more likely to bump into things physically or conflict with others.

Positive intention carries us over the long haul and helps us through rough times. Combined with a sense of purpose, it is intention that keeps us moving through doubt, opposition, and failure. By learning to master intent, we increase our chances of success and fulfillment of purpose. If we fail to master intent, we run the risk of having our victimhood unconsciously dominate our lives.

TARANEH: FACING VICTIMHOOD

Taraneh is a Milwaukee resident whose story is one in progress. Her struggle with intent continues as she strives to grow her business, which is the playing field where she faces her victimhood and learns mastery of intent.

Taraneh's life had been one of feast or famine. She sold home improvements, like additions, windows, remodeling. For Taraneh, selling was no problem. Her close rates were among the highest in her industry. When she needed money, she went out and sold. When she didn't, she didn't. That's why her employer was willing to keep her on through the bad times.

Taraneh had a whole encyclopedia of excuses for her erratic performance. They included the weather, buying cycles, the economy, discontent with suppliers, her boss. . . . Taraneh blamed her employer so often and came to believe her own reasoning sufficiently that she finally quit to go out on her own. "He's my biggest problem—why give that old so and so the biggest piece of the pie?" Under this reasoning, Taraneh fantasized that with "more of the pie," she would not have to work as hard.

Taraneh's father had been an alcoholic county road worker in rural Wisconsin. He demonstrated for Taraneh that work was a battle to minimize effort and avoid work as much as possible. Taraneh knew this was mistaken but still carried these reactive intentions in her unconscious.

On days of low excuses and high productivity, she wondered to herself how much of her early training influenced her feast-or-famine pattern. She repeatedly brushed the thought away. That didn't matter anymore, because she would be working for herself soon. Things would all be different. And they were—for the first three months she was in business.

When she went out on her own it was spring, and Taraneh sold up a storm. Things were much harder than she'd imagined. She lost a few bids because she couldn't get materials at the high volume discount of her former employer. Her supplier relations got more complicated. She was in charge of her own installation and construction crews, and the problems of delivery kept getting in the way of sales.

It seemed that the better she did, the more she suffered. But she'd had a great spring, so she figured she'd go mountain climbing for a week. When she came back, she couldn't seem to get in gear. There was always something wrong with the house to fix, the kids needed her at home. Her "vacation" continued through the fall, and Taraneh had failed to get moving again. That's about when she came in for some coaching. If she blew the fall, she knew she would never make it.

With some difficulty, Taraneh uncovered her sense of victimhood and shame. She realized that success was contrary to what she had learned at home. Her deep-seated negative attitudes about work caused her to discount her peak sales experiences. The more successful she was, the more sorry she felt for herself.

Csikszentmihalyi, in *Flow*, addresses this phenomenon. He points out that by far the greatest proportion of flow we experience is at work, yet Americans as a group insist on regarding work negatively. Taraneh was no exception. It seemed she just couldn't have it too good. That's when she began to realize that intent was what determined her highs and lows—not the weather, the market, and so on.

She began focusing on positive intent and overcame the reactive intent that made her work seasonal. She had a great December and January, the months when she'd told herself before that nobody would buy. She gave off-season discounts to make these sales, but still her beliefs of victimhood were shaken. Her positive intent was carrying her through. The responsibility of no boss and realizing that blame just kept her stuck helped Taraneh begin to taste the mastery of intent.

She still has a long way to go. For two years, she has consistently broken out of the seasonal cycles that kept her trapped, and the last three years have been her best ever. She's smoothed out the feast-or-famine pattern a lot and is structuring the coming year to give herself rewards each month for meeting her goals. As soon as they are met, she gets to take the rest of the month off or accrue dollars for future rewards.

The mastery of intent is a lifelong pursuit that requires honoring negative intent and transforming it to the direct service of our higher purposes. We're all like Taraneh in some way, and the adventure of mastery is open to each of us, regardless of the ways our victimhood and shame limit us. Be it at home, work, or elsewhere, by honoring ourselves as creators of our own lives, we can shed the light of consciousness in the darker corners of our unconscious victimhood and discover the raw power of intent to be harnessed in the service of our higher purposes. With victimhood, we are at the mercy of a world run and crafted by others. With intention, we are masters of a world we create. **(AMP)***

---

* AMP 1—Identify an example of negative intention-i.e., an intention that is reactive and/or works against your positive purpose. What were you reacting against? What was the positive intent of your behavior?

* AMP 2—Identify three to five instances where negative intention adversely affected your career. Imagine how you could channel that energy in each case into positive intent that would support your higher purpose.

* AMP 3—Identify three examples where you reacted in anger to a situation or person. Were you able to channel your energy toward positive purpose? If so, how? If not, why not?

TRUTH

It makes all the difference in the world whether we put truth in the first place, or in second place.

...JOHN MORLEY

A workplace with a full flow of truth is a highly engaged environment if top-quality, timely communication takes place—where the right hand knows what the left hand is doing and both hands work in harmony and full power. It is also likely to be an environment of high purpose fulfillment.

Expression of truth to our highest vision is the pathfinder, triangulating between head, heart, and our world, the way the explorer uses sun, time, and mountains to tell where he is going. It is our best indicator of the path of purpose. Truth is aliveness in relationship to a group. Belonging to the peer group is especially important in adolescence. Expression of truth to our highest vision is the principle at this stage of development. According to Dr. G. Michael Durst, author of *Napkin Notes on the Art of Living*, eighty percent of the population never makes it through this level of development to a point where they can fully express what they think and feel. As we saw with Tony as we considered aliveness, fear of rejection keeps significant parts of most people hidden from others, even our most beloved. This leads to a workplace and loving relationships operating without the benefit of each person's fullest or real perspective. Full power and satisfaction remain unavailable.

In a workplace where individuals freely express their highest truth, we are more likely to see constantly improving product and means of production. Teams fire on all cylinders, and the organization performs optimally. Information flows to where it is needed, there are fewer surprises, and the problems that do arise are met with more orchestrated, effective responses.

More than most of us would like to admit, we live our lives seeing things we don't like and ignoring them. We go through our lives thinking thoughts and keeping them to ourselves. We

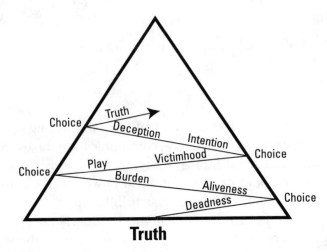

Figure 7.5

get furious at other drivers and yell heartily from our glassy co-
coon, but when we meet face to face we are meek and mild or
distant and steaming. Even when we do finally show true feelings of anger, they are usually ineffective for true fulfillment because we have built an unmanageable backlog, submerging
much fear and hurt in the process. This is what Dr. Deepak
Chopra calls "fragmented living." He tells stories of patients
who come to see him, break down in sobs, rage, fear, and guilt,
then compose themselves leaving cheerily. He gives them the
opportunity to get in touch with and release their feelings and
they feel better.

   We aren't in tune with our deepest feelings anywhere near
as well as we could be. Worse yet, our families and the places we
work suffer because we withhold often useful information, as
we repress the expression of truth. We often withhold our best
for fear of rejection. Valuable information is not shared, and our
fullest involvement is withheld. Fulfillment is unavailable. Both
the love of family and productivity at work are limited. Companies continue making the same mistakes because employees
knowingly look on. Our loved ones don't get our best, and,
sadly, neither do we.

BE GENUINE—FOLLOW TRUTH

I speak the truth, not so much as I would, but as much as I dare; and I dare a little more as I grow older.

...MONTAIGNE

Expression of truth to our highest vision causes us to wake up. It can be seen as a journey into the lands of shame and deception in each of us. Each truth responsibly expressed leads us into new uncharted territories of increasing integrity. By releasing one view, we are able to experience others. We discover deeper and more complete realities within and without. Our pictures of the world and experiences of life grow and become richer as we follow the path of our truth. We grow in skill and substance and move more rapidly towards our highest purpose fulfillment.

We call it the truth to our "highest vision," because as we grow and mature, our perspective changes. It is not simply fact but the most complete representation of our perspective we can muster. By following it we face our fears, heal our hurts, and apply ourselves with full intent. Full expression of truth ultimately leads to purpose fulfillment. Many of us fail to express the truth of what is going on inside us because we are embarrassed. We are afraid we will embarrass ourselves by some expression that doesn't conform, or we fear we will fail to express our highest vision. This is often so because previously withheld expression causes our highest to be laden with unexpressed anger, guilt, and blame. Deception is the polarity of truth, and we all deceive in some ways. Overcoming fear of full expression is a part of most paths of higher purpose. When we withhold, we deceive. Often we deceive ourselves as well. We limit our consciousness or awareness.

When we withhold our truth, we keep ourselves and the world around us from growing. Growth means change, and change can be scary. The truth to our highest vision is forever changing and regularly takes us into unknown, uncomfortable territory, especially at work, where our livelihood is at stake.

Fortunately, it also provides the compass to guide us in the un-known.

"You don't withhold the truth?" some will say. It is the cour-age to express the truth more and more fully that marks our in-tegrity, not some absolute standard. We are talking neither about overt lying nor irresponsible criticism but the full courageous manifestation of our truest selves. Even the most forthright truth-tellers have withheld hidden areas of doubt, shame, and victim-hood within themselves, regardless of their corporate or personal positions. If any of us can say we are absolutely truthful, we are either saints or deeply asleep to our fullest experience.

Even the rich, famous, and powerful withhold the truth of their experiences, to the detriment of their corporations. In my work with various executives at major Fortune 500 companies, I have been surprised at the amount of self-deception, excuse making, buck passing, and blame evident at all levels of the company. One client in particular was a multibillion-dollar fam-ily-founded business. Even though its stock was publicly traded, it was still run as a kingdom—the heir apparent repre-senting the third generation of family leadership.

The father was chairman of the board. He had run the com-pany until turning over the reins to a professional manager to oversee until his son was ready to take over.

The president spoke to me one day about the irresponsibil-ity, victimhood, and poor performance of his subordinates. After a few probing questions, he was soon also complaining about how his hands were tied by the chairman. The reform he wanted was thwarted. As I questioned further, however, it became clear that the president had rarely, and only tentatively, mentioned his dissatisfaction to the chairman.

As the conversation turned back to the president and his staff, I observed that it was no surprise his staff complained irre-sponsibly, since he operated the same way. They withheld their truth from him just as he withheld his from the chairman. He took exception to this, so I recounted the conversation, demon-strating his victimhood. Within the next week, each vice presi-dent and division president was asked about his or her discontent. All denied it, too afraid to express directly the feelings they regularly leaked to others. They were just like the president.

Most of these executives were Ivy League MBAs from wealthy families, making well over a half a million dollars each year. A good number of them were independently wealthy. If people in this position, with this kind of worldly security and power, are afraid to express the truth to their highest vision, imagine what it must be like for the rest of us to face the fear of losing a job and acceptance.

FOLLOWING THE TRUTH THROUGH AUTHORITY BARRIERS

For my part, whatever anguish of spirit it may cost, I am willing to know the whole truth—to know the worst and provide for it.

...PATRICK HENRY

Authority issues are one of the major barriers to expressing truth. The president and chairman of the board of this multibillion-dollar firm had not resolved their issues with authority. As a result, full truth, alignment, and power were not available to them. Most of us have attitudes about authority that cause us to rebel, submit, or passively resist. Few of us express our truth fully and move easily and fully into partnership with authority, no matter how high our own position. Fewer still engage in direct, honest communication with peers or subordinates, for that matter.

Robert Paul, or RP, is an engineering genius. He routinely takes over failing divisions and turns them around through his considerable abilities, which range from production management to organization structuring and sales.

RP was born (in his own words) to "poor white trash." His father returned from World War II a broken man, drinking heavily, hating the Germans and everyone else, including his family, all of whom he blamed for his problems. Whether he was in a drunken rage or not, he beat RP mercilessly. Only when the family doctor recognized RP's superior intelligence and had him tested was he taken from his abusive environment, made a ward of the state, and placed in foster care, from which he attended schools for the gifted.

RP's intelligence carried him easily through school to an engineering degree from MIT. Rising quickly through the manufacturing ranks, he became a top manager with a reputation so strong that he eventually became a highly paid "hired gun," a corporate turnaround artist who could take a business from losing to top profit in just a few years.

He worked his artistry over and over for various corporations but never made a home until he decided to get personal coaching. He figured he was moving into the last assignment of his career and wanted to develop a nourishing home life at some company rather than riding off into the sunset to the next challenge.

When he began examining his past with the intention of shifting his future, he discovered he had rarely taken a second assignment with the same corporation, and if he did, he shifted his reporting relationship. He had, in fact, left companies purposely because of what he viewed as the general "gross incompetence of top-level American management."

In every assignment, RP had been at odds with top corporate-level management, his division pitted not only against the marketplace and itself but against "the rampant stupidity of corporate number crunchers"—an extra weight he felt he had to bear. RP, you see, did not trust authority. He prided himself on the open atmosphere he created with his employees but did not believe that "corporate bean counters" could handle the truth from him.

Authority issues were seriously in the way of RP's ultimate goal of finding a happy corporate home to finish out his career. His biggest barrier was telling the truth to his superiors. He did battle when necessary and was considered a malcontent by many, but he never aligned in full production and planning outside his division. He met goals and expectations but never got "to be left in peace." He was alone in a hostile world, within and without. He let his judgments of his superiors keep him from communicating the information they needed to know and help him. As a result, they invariably became part of his perceived enemy. One of the first things he needed to do was get his feelings about authority cleared up. He recognized his earliest childhood experiences of authority as coming from an "incompetent mother" and an abusive father.

He saw how his lack of alignment with venture capitalists and corporate conglomerates came at least in part from his earliest feelings of distrust and disrespect of authority. Once he got this knee-jerk antiauthority reaction out of the way, he reduced the emotional charge that caused him to be so critical of authority. He began to see individuals in positions of responsibility more clearly. He sorted out the ones who wanted to know and were genuinely interested from those who lived lives of threatened functionaries.

He increasingly began to get the ear of the chairman and dealt with some very dicey situations in cooperation with holding company officers for the first time. Several serious trade infringements and other issues arose, giving him reason to move into deeper partnership than he'd ever imagined. He began planning and strategizing with the chairman and accepted that those not as gifted as he could still be valuable allies and confederates in the pursuit of the corporation's higher purpose. He began experiencing high praise for his radical restructuring and aggressive marketing plans.

As of this writing, the entire company is watching his progress and the innovations he is implementing, with the intention of following his lead and adopting his methodologies. He has overcome his authority issues sufficiently to tell his superiors truths and opinions he would never have disclosed. As a result, he has begun experiencing at least part of the belonging and partnership he wanted in his last assignment.

Formerly, RP expressed himself and repelled others. This was no more his true and highest expression than those of us who withhold expression because of fear of rejection and issues with authority. Regardless of our error, whether over- or under-expression, expression of truth to our highest vision takes us into and reveals the issues that stand in the way of our higher purpose fulfillment.

Authority and other personal issues diminish the full expression of truth and communication between employees and employers at all levels of American business. Line workers give up on telling the truth to their supervisors and middle managers, who are often withholding themselves all around too. Some go home and complain, and some go to the club to distract themselves. At any rate, individuals and firms alike suffer from lack of the sweet, healing, growth-promoting expression of truth; truth we need to progress fully on our path of purpose.

This is not to say that all authority embraces the truth or that subordinates express it particularly well, but the truth from a committed, responsible, high-performing employee is a valuable commodity that any top executive with integrity should be willing if not glad to hear. Remember, executives have vulnerabilities too: presenting the truth effectively requires a great deal of skill. We must be responsible and learn graceful ways to deliver hard truths if we are to continue to grow and develop. The path can be rough, but the growth in effectiveness and purpose fulfillment ultimately proves worthwhile. If people at your company don't want to hear your truth and you are responsible and high-performing, stay true. You may have outgrown this environment. Plenty of other places need your unique contributions.

FEAR OF OURSELVES

The man who fears no truths has nothing to fear from lies.
...THOMAS JEFFERSON

Failure to express our truth fully slows purpose fulfillment. Perhaps the greatest barrier to our full expression of the truth is ourselves. I'm often amused and appalled by the number of people who tell their boss off *after* being fired. This isn't expression of truth to our highest vision, it is irresponsible dumping. Besides that, most of those I know who claim to have "told him where to get off" are much bolder in the retelling than the telling itself. We either don't know how to express our truth responsibly or don't care to express it that way. We'd rather blame than reach for the most responsible expression—it's easier and helps us avoid the work responsibility might imply. Blame is rarely our highest, most responsible expression since we all know deep down that we are more responsible for our own experience than we generally want to acknowledge.

Most of us would rather complain to others and be somewhat unhappy than engage in the more purposeful journey of expressing the truth to our highest vision. Expression is inconvenient and gives us more dragons to face. We must confront our lack of commitment and others' denial. We must repeatedly move through conflict to harmony until, ultimately, we claim our reward: more work and responsibility. In expressing truth to our highest vision we face skill defects in personal responsibility and communication effectiveness. The most important facts can be obscured by a poor or tainted delivery. The good news is that we don't have to hold back so much; we can feel more alive, conscious, and at peace with ourselves as we move toward our highest purpose.

It's not only fear of rejection that keeps us from expressing the truth of our experience to our highest vision. Most of us have sat in meetings where someone comes up with a good idea. What happens? He or she gets the job of doing it. Irresponsibility or the desire to watch others fail cause us to hold our tongues—we know we'd get more work and risk failure if we spoke up.

The path indicated by the expression of truth to our highest vision is unpredictable. It draws more and more out of us, leading us deeper into ourselves and our worlds. It presents great hazards and the greatest reward of all. It leads us to our highest self and, ultimately, to fulfillment of our highest purpose. Along the way we grow, get hurt, heal, and come to peace with ourselves and our world. Commitment to following our truth carries us through the dark times to our brightest light, our finest, highest, and truest selves. **(AMP)***

COMMITMENT

> *Until one is committed there is hesitancy, the chance to draw back, always ineffectiveness.*
>
> *Concerning all acts of initiative (and creation) there is one elementary truth, the ignorance of which kills countless ideas and splendid plans: the moment that one definitely commits one's self then Providence moves too.*
>
> *All sorts of things occur to help one that would otherwise never have occurred. A whole stream of events issues from the decision, raising in one's favor all manner of unforeseen incidents and meetings and material assistance, which no man or woman could have dreamt would have come his way. Whatever you can do or dream you can—begin it. Boldness has genius, power, and magic in it.***

Thomas Jefferson is quoted in the unabridged Oxford English Dictionary for first use of the word "commitment" as we define it here: "an unreserved and open commitment to measures of reform." For us, the key term is "unreserved and open." Commitment can be to reform, a goal or higher purpose. We need to follow this principle for our ultimate purpose fulfillment.

In committed corporate life there is more likely to be joyous sharing of the yoke of service. There is certainty in each other— the cracks things would normally fall through are watched by many with the dedication of commitment. One plus one equals three as corporate synergy results.

Commitment is aliveness in dedicated life direction. It requires perseverance in aliveness and direction. With commit-

---

* AMP—Identify one to three examples of times you took a risk in expressing the truth, even though you feared negative consequences to yourself or others. A) What was one fear you had to overcome in each case? B) What were the results of your truth telling? C) How did this risk-taking support your life purpose?
** Goethe in *Breakpoint and Beyond*, ed. Land and Jarman, (New York: Harper Business, 1992)

ment, we dedicate ourselves to larger, longer-term goals, outcomes, or ways of being. This dedication causes us to face barriers we would otherwise have avoided. In young adulthood, commitment leads us on our journey through life. With it we face personal barriers, learn, grow, and mature into full expression of purpose. Some commit to higher ideals, others to accomplishment alone, and still others put the two together.

Avoidance is the polarity to commitment. With avoidance come lack of fulfillment and resentment. Avoidance limits our development, service, and, ultimately, our purpose fulfillment. Companies with a large quota of uncommitted employees are less productive, creative, and competitive.

On the other hand, a committed work force means greater service and growth all around. We grow through commitments, learning the skills we need to fulfill our aims and overcoming our own barriers in order to succeed. Committed people develop character through their unreserved focus on their highest aim.

Attaining our aims through committed action, we strive and often find our life purpose. Sometimes we discover our purpose by realizing it is not furthered by our current commitment. Other times we find it deeply imbedded in our original

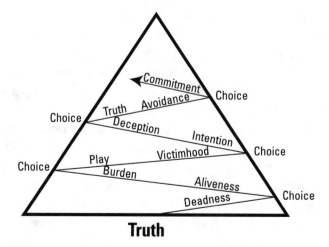

Figure 7.6

aims—striving with commitment, we find the heart of our purpose. Ideally, our purpose and commitments become ever more closely attuned throughout our careers.

COMMITMENT AND FOLLOW-THROUGH: FROM A REACTIVE TO A CREATIVE LIFE

Hakeem was born poor. Hunger was his daily childhood companion, and he dedicated his adult life to never experiencing the pain of hunger again. His commitment to wealth and financial security was very strong. He worked his way through his country's equivalent of high school and maintained a full workload during college, where he studied finance. Hakeem learned the banking industry inside out, becoming a bank bailout specialist. Throughout the '70s and early '80s, he would put a group of investors together, buy a bank, release nonperforming staff, let go of bad business, and focus the organization fully on profit.

By the time Hakeem was forty-five he had sufficient reserves never to know hunger in the course of everyday life for many lifetimes. He had also been through two marriages and earned the resentment of his children. He claimed to be baffled by their feelings, since he had "given them everything money could buy." The extreme nature of his life commitment precluded understanding why his children felt this way.

After all, they had never had to worry about eating or other desires, so why weren't they grateful? Hakeem had just sold a savings and loan bank for a big profit to his investors and himself. He had millions set aside for retirement as well as several million dollars at hand for his next venture.

He was confused by his failure to move on several good opportunities. It was at this point that Hakeem came in to see me for a consultation. As we talked, it became clear that Hakeem's life was about the pursuit of money. This commitment was absolute. He started hustling early in grade school and had worked legitimate jobs since he was twelve years old.

Hakeem, as it turns out, had never experienced anything resembling a family life or a secure childhood. It is hardly any wonder he could not comprehend his family's complaints.

While discussing life purpose, Hakeem came up blank at first, finally he began to see the problem, even shedding a few tears at his feeling of despair around a life of higher purpose. He reported these to be his first tears since childhood. He had accomplished all of his life goals but felt empty. His children and former wives reviled him, and he knew something was wrong. The good news is that his commitment carried him through to this level of questioning, so he could see the limitation of his commitment and his need for more.

Hakeem realized that in intending to leave his past and pain behind, he had left his family and himself behind too. Healing his family, nurturing himself, and helping others became central to Hakeem's sense of purpose. His new commitment to his higher purpose included his own happiness, the health of his family, and the good of his community. He went into therapy with his ex-wives and children, began hearing their complaints, and delivered some of his own.

He and his estranged son began relating and doing things together. Professionally, Hakeem began teaching business and finance at local colleges, working as a consultant to help struggling businesses he believed in. He'd reoriented his commitment from a full stomach to a life of fulfillment by following his newly clarified purpose: to help others know the abundance that comes with togetherness and love, his new hungers.

Whether we are like Hakeem, whose commitment helped him see where he didn't want to go and change direction, or like Stan, whose story showed him looking deeper into his life and finding an intense sense of purpose in the direction he was already going, commitment will lead us to our purpose if we engage honestly.

Intention is key to the focus and follow-through of commitment, but play helps us engage joyfully, and aliveness animates the whole process. As we live by the principles of purpose, up to and including commitment, we develop an increasing sense of mastery and meaning. Our lives become more powerfully purposeful, and we grow in responsibility. **(AMP)***

RESPONSIBILITY

> *The truth is simple: we are responsible for everything in our experience whether we like it or not. Liking or not liking the situation are only evaluations.*
>
> ...G. M. DURST

Fully responsible corporations exist in our ideals only. In them, we radiate purpose and blame is an infrequent visitor. Synergy leads to creative, effective responses to the needs of clients, employees, community, humanity, and to planetary well-being. In the responsible corporation, each learns his or her lessons with grace and expresses the highest levels of love, truth, and compassion available.

Responsibility means claiming full authority for our lives. It is commitment in our way of being, aliveness in existence. With responsibility, we assume all credit or blame for gaps between our stated ideals and actual behavior. We are clearly creators of our own reality: responsible living is alive, playful, intentional, truthful, and committed. We acknowledge our shortcomings and act purposefully to fulfill our ideals; blaming others for who we are and what we do is no longer an option.

Blame is the polarity of responsibility and refers to guilt and accusation. Responsibility blames neither ourselves nor others. As responsible people, we are full authors of our reality. Blame is one of the major barriers to assuming responsibility. Blame dwells in culpability, while responsibility acknowledges choice and creation. Accusing others or turning inward in self-

---

* Identify three major committments in your life. How have these commitments been challenged? How did your response to the challenge deepen your committment and sense of life purpose?

hate or guilt is not responsibility. Responsibility simply acknowledges what's so and makes appropriate adjustments.

The norm for most of us is to some extent to blame the world for our shortcomings. We do this because we have difficulty accepting ourselves as creators of our own experience. In the workplace, this takes the form of passing the buck, making excuses, and so on. The result? Lowered fulfillment, effectiveness, and productivity. Imagine the opposite: work teams of one-hundred-percent-responsible members. Problems would be solved quickly and creatively, everyone keeping an eye on the future to exploit opportunities and avoid trouble. Resistance to service and to innovation would be unknown as the corporation evolves in exquisite response to the needs of its many constituencies.

Blame is irresponsibility. From the irresponsible position, I am more the victim than the author of my own existence. I do not consistently keep my word, live up to implied agreements, and take action, hiding in a cloud of excuses. Irresponsibility and blame are the bane of much corporate and business life. With them, the buck is passed, commitments are not made or met, the truth is not told, and resistance is the order of the day in an environment of burden and fear cloaked in hostility.

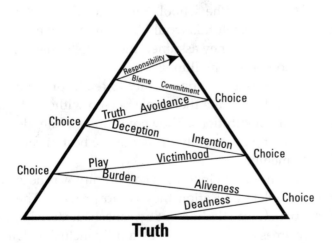

Figure 7.7

We are all in some stage of climbing out of this nightmarish existence toward our highest selves. As on a coin with two sides, we can each choose the responsible, alive way of existing over and over.

FACE IT—OWN IT—BE TRANSFORMED

It is easy to dodge our responsibilities, but we cannot dodge the consequences of dodging our responsibilities.

...E. C. McKenzie

One of the oldest colleges in the Midwest is Shimer College, originally a religious school, which developed into an ideal-driven avant-garde educational institution. It serves bright exceptional students in a community environment that helps even the most rebellious and those in need of extra nurturing to succeed.

In the late 1970s, an Episcopal priest named Don Moon, who had originally been a physicist, came to teach at the college, finding its cause a compelling way to unify his love of God and science. The church subsequently withdrew its sponsorship of the college, and the beautiful campus in Mount Carroll, Illinois, became increasingly difficult to maintain. In the end, the directors decided to close the school. Several of the teachers and a number of students felt this would be an intolerable loss, so under Don's leadership they assumed the school's charter, moving the campus to Waukegan, Illinois.

They saw this as an opportunity to reinterpret the school's mission, to really educate the whole person without the lip service of so many institutions. They envisioned a fully democratic community that would really draw out the best in each student and faculty member.

They felt full participation in community was necessary for the most complete education they could provide. The ideal of full participation was fleshed out by consensus decision-making in as many areas as possible and by a fully inclusive democratic process throughout. Their intent was to develop a curriculum that integrated students meaningfully into the life of a campus that was a truly inclusive community. The intent was to educate all in every aspect of management and decision making.

Students learned foundations of the cutting-edge thinking of their culture and were prepared for careers and lives of full, meaningful participation in their communities as adults. The bright student who needed extra attention thrived in this environment of inclusion and respect. Everyone's voice was valued, and all received a complete hearing on their concerns. There was always time enough to give the caring needed. The faculty saw to this.

The school's growth was tough. Its existence was in question for several years. It had lost accreditation and funding when it left Mount Carroll. Funding and students were hard to come by. The dedication and responsibility of those first faculty and students was extreme. The faculty were all paid the same minimal wage, and for this they not only taught but performed all the administrative functions of the school. If they had failed to take full responsibility during this tough transition time, as so many do, the academic world would be much poorer, having lost one of the most clearly ideal-driven academic institutions in the country.

Fortunately they persevered, and little by little, more students came, buildings were added, and accreditation was regained. Overseas programs developed, and the school began to flourish. The staff grew, and the old democratic form became unwieldy. They were faced with yet another opportunity for responsible change.

They evolved new ways of decision making to honor their original ideals of inclusion and to respect all members of the community while allowing more efficiency in operations. These current forms do not compromise but enhance the original mission and ideals. The vision of a fully educated member of society has continued to expand. Quality of relationship, self-esteem, social conscience, knowledge base, and ability to live with full heart are held as high as or higher than ever as the school follows its destiny.

The personal responsibility of Don Moon throughout this evolution has been an inspiration. Blame is not a major part of his operating mode—he accepts the school's problems as a reflection of his own personal issues and challenges, and acts accordingly. As president, he is willing to be held accountable for his embodiment of the school's ideals by the faculty, board of directors, and students.

He knows he is an evolving human being with gaps between his ideals and reality, and he works diligently to narrow these. His personal adventure continues internally and externally, in the spiritual and the mundane. He has the same problems we all face, but he has learned to live with increasing consonance to the principle of responsibility, and his school benefits because of it. It demonstrates responsibility as the road to healthy individuals, organizations, and society. **(AMP)***

THEY ALL FIT

From this perspective, we can look back and see that responsibility is impossible without commitment, and commitment without truth is limited. Intention provides the power behind expression of truth to our highest vision, and play provides the foundation for intention. Aliveness runs clearly through all these, leading us to our highest purpose.

From this perspective, purpose is an alive adventure of nourishment and fulfillment that flows from our intent and is a profound expression of our deepest truth to our highest vision. Our commitment and personal responsibility will, in the end, give our purposeful lives an integrated, joyful quality and an attractive richness. Purposeful living makes our daily lives sparkle—nothing need be ordinary again.

---

* AMP—What are your specific challenges to taking full responsibility for your company or organization? What leads you to stop short of full responsibility? What would it take for you to assume a higher level of responsibility in your current job?

Living by these principles of purpose, we "transform" from our lowest to our highest selves. For this reason, we also call them the principles of transformation. Furthermore, by living "on purpose" and with responsibility, we learn to live and do business from the *transcendental* principles. Transcendental principles flow from our highest selves. They include love, grace, acceptance, compassion, and others. To experience and live these is at the root of all highest purpose, whether articulated as such or not.

There is no polarity to the transcendental principles. At this level, we are unified in our existence. We *are* our commitment and purpose. From this perspective, we see business as a playground where we develop ourselves, learning our lessons and becoming our most loving, compassionate selves.

The principles of purpose provide the rungs of the ladder to these heights. After all, what would love be without aliveness or play? How could we be fully loving without full conscious intent and truth? It is impossible to imagine love without commitment and purpose. Each day of our business lives is an opportunity to practice using the principles of higher purpose: tools of love and ultimate caring.

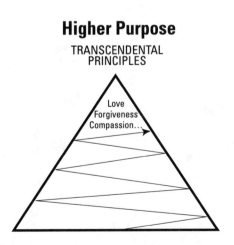

Figure 7.8

I recently proposed to a group of European bankers that daily service was an opportunity to express love, and they turned their noses up at this proposition. Love, they said, was good, but how could I equate it to banking? When I asked them if they were not loving in serving, what, then, were they doing? I received shrugs of impatience. Whether you buy this hypothesis of business as love or not, try it and ask yourself, "If not love, what?" You need not accept this hypothesis to live true to the principles of purpose. Fear, burden, victimhood, deception, avoidance, and blame drag all of us down to some extent. Likewise, they provide the opportunity for us to employ the principles of purpose and move toward our highest.

In Don Moon's purpose, we see the love of higher purpose in action. Each of the lessons he learns as a priest and president of Shimer helps him drop illusion, focus on the truth, hone his commitment, and improve the level of his responsibility.

Top organizational functioning provides the most playful, alive, intentional, genuine, committed environment possible for staff and students. In short, they are well loved, learning better and better to love. In this kind of environment we will most likely grow to our highest.

We now move on to examine the requirements for a life of full purpose.

Chapter 8

Living a Life of Purpose:
Beyond Time Management

Never forget that life can only be nobly inspired and rightly lived if you take it bravely and gallantly, as a splendid adventure in which you are setting out into an unknown country to face many a danger, to meet many a joy, to find many a comrade, to win and lose many a battle.

...ANNIE BESANT

We have seen how the skills of time management are useful and, in many cases, necessary, but they are not sufficient for us to perform to our best in the many spheres where we operate. This is especially true over the long haul. In time management, the goal is to get more done in less time. Without purpose, the accomplishments of the excellent time manager lack full power, being relatively hollow both in scope and impact. Furthermore, accomplishment will be limited—alignment and empowerment from others and the environment will be diminished. Purpose and vision are invaluable if not necessary for the long-term maintenance of top performance and accomplishment.

We have seen how purpose maximizes flow, personal performance, and numerous other aspects of accomplishment and fulfillment. We have also seen that purpose is a difficult abstraction to apply. The principles of purpose provide more accessible tools that we can apply daily in any situation with relative ease.

Focusing on these principles provides an accessible tool, an immediate objective, much as we focus on the yellow lines in the middle of the road when driving in fog. We can't see our larger destination, but we keep focused and moving, using centerlines for orientation. However, if we didn't need to be somewhere, we might just pack it in and not bother to drive through the fog. Purpose provides the motivation to keep us going. Just as we drive more quickly and persistently when we must be somewhere, purpose draws us forward through life's uncertainties.

REQUIREMENTS FOR LIVING A LIFE OF PURPOSE

There are three key requirements to living a life of purpose. They are *courage*, *perseverance*, and *learning and growing*. We need to have the *courage* to really say what matters to us and take the risks that move us ahead. We need *perseverance* to keep going, and we must *learn* so we develop the skills and become the person needed to fulfill our purpose.

COURAGE

> *Courage is rightly esteemed the first of human qualities because it is the quality which guarantees all others.*
>
> ...WINSTON CHURCHILL

First of all, we need the courage to declare a significant ultimate destination. In following this vision, we render ourselves vulnerable to the pain of failure and the scoffing of those who are less committed. We also need to have the courage to face the truth of our shortcomings in order to continue learning, and we need courage to keep growing toward our ultimate purpose fulfillment.

Just as courage is necessary to drive in the fog, courage is necessary in business with purpose. We must have the courage to tell the truth about how things are and what really matters to us, the courage to face our wounds and the courage to face displeasure and negative outcomes. We must dare to play a bigger game. With higher purpose, the home runs become more challenging and the play more demanding. The bottom line expands, and success takes on new meaning. Profit is no longer measured only as the surplus cash left over at the end of the day. It becomes a much more demanding measure of satisfaction and contribution: satisfaction of our basic needs and contribution to all our fellow business participants and our communities.

PERSEVERANCE

> *The most important thing in the Olympic games is not to win but to take part, just as the most important thing in life is not the triumph but the struggle. The essential thing is not to have conquered but to have fought well.*
>
> ...BARON DE COUBERTIN, MODERN OLYMPICS FOUNDER

For us to succeed over the long haul, purpose requires not only the courage to risk losing comforts and gaining disapproval, but also constancy and *perseverance*. Without *perseverance*, we risk meandering meaninglessly from one good idea or project to another. We more readily get distracted or give up, and our purpose becomes a disempowering indictment rather than a compelling beacon as we deviate.

Abraham Lincoln's perseverance was remarkable. I can still remember the long list of elections he lost on his way to the presidency. In later years, I became aware of the incredible perseverance of Helen Keller and her teacher, Anne Sullivan. In the face of infant blindness and deafness, Helen developed not only language but a life that contributed significantly to our society.

LEARNING AND GROWING

> *Courage is the basic virtue for everyone so long as he continues to grow, to move ahead; it is, as Ellen Glasgow remarks, "the only lasting virtue."*
>
> ...ROLLO MAY

A worthy purpose carries challenges with it, or it wouldn't be worthy. Raising children, succeeding at marriage, and completing a career of integrity and contribution—all hold innumerable challenges that require our perseverance. Purpose is not a one-time fix but a conceptual tool that draws us forward into and through the adventure of our lives. While our perseverance keeps us engaged in the adventure, we must *learn and grow* to progress, so that we can develop as fully as possible. Those who persevere in their purpose develop skills beyond those of similar capacities who do not.

Most of us want to find the magic bullet that will help us avoid future hurts and problems. There is no such thing, nor should there be. We are all here to learn and grow toward our highest potential, and only the continual application of ourselves to this end causes us to become our highest self. Business, marriage, and parenthood provide some of the most exquisite "schooling" in which we can learn our lessons and become the finest selves we can be. If we found the magic bullet, we would miss out on the magic of developing ourselves fully.

The sooner we accept the lifelong role of students, the sooner we quit looking for quick fixes and apply ourselves to learning and growing to our utmost. Marsha learned this with her investing clients and left behind a world of constant tension for one of mutual discovery, adventure, and learning with her clients. As she learned and grew, her life came together.

Purpose does indeed help us move beyond time management into much higher realms of accomplishment. Accomplishment becomes compelling and necessary for us to reach our highest and be our best: the best parents, partners, workers, and members of the human family we can be. Purpose brings out the finest in us as human beings.

The life of Russell Conwell exemplifies, in my opinion, our highest in courage, perseverance, and learning.

A Man of Purpose

Biographer Robert Shackleton tells us Conwell was born in 1843 and lived until 1925. He was born into a poor farming family, where he began to learn how to lead a life of purpose from his parents. As a young child he was exposed to visitors like abolitionist John Brown and orator Frederick Douglass. Brown came to hide from the authorities. Douglass, no doubt, came out of the common purpose of freedom that was the goal of all workers on the underground railway, which ran through Conwell's house. At an early age, he helped transport escaping slaves with his father. He was learning about the caring that goes with higher purpose, witnessing his father's attempt to sell his farm to raise legal defense fees for Brown prior to Brown's execution.

Community Service

Community service was such a large part of Conwell's life that he repeatedly left college to serve in the War between the States, and his father sent him back. His father finally relented and allowed him to join his childhood friends in the Civil War. His dedication to his community, in the Berkshire mountains of Massachusetts, was so strong that at nineteen, when he enlisted for the second time, numerous others from his community joined too, insisting that he be made captain of their unit. His youth required a special commission from the governor of the state.

Conwell completed his military service as a colonel, having consistently risked his own life for the lives of his men. His men, in turn, risked all for their young leader. The death of one of his loyal men changed Conwell's life dramatically. His men had given him a sword inscribed "True friendship is eternal." John Ring, his aide-de-camp, was especially proud of this memento. John was his aide because he was too small and underdeveloped to enlist as a regular.

Conwell recounts how their position was overrun by a surprise Confederate attack. His men immediately retreated across a river, setting fire to the covered bridge over which they had escaped. The firing across the river was intense, and no one noticed Ring, who had gone back to Conwell's tent to reclaim the sword. John began running across the bridge into the flames. The Confederates called for him to return. A Confederate officer even waved a white flag stopping the firing and called his assurance that John would be allowed to rejoin his group. But the appeal was too late; John had already entered the covered part of the bridge.

John emerged in flames himself minutes later, sword in hand, to cheers from both sides. Sadly, he was already so badly burned that he died giving his final message to Conwell, who later wrote, "When I stood beside the body of John Ring and realized that he had died for love of me . . . I vowed that from that moment I would live not only my own life, but that I would also live the life of John Ring. And from that moment I have worked sixteen hours every day—eight for John's work and eight hours of my own. . . . Every morning when I rise I look at this sword . . . or think of the sword, and vow anew . . . ."

Conwell used the sword like a statement of purpose to keep himself on track in his life—and what a life he led. He made and lost significant amounts of money, was biographer to most presidents of the U.S. in his lifetime, started the first YMCA in the town in Minneapolis, the first free school for former slave children, and hospitals and churches. He was an author, teacher, lecturer, newspaper publisher, and a very successful attorney.

It was in his capacity as attorney that his life began to take one of its most definitive turns. He was advising an older woman about the disposal of a ramshackle old church with a tiny, shrinking congregation. In his meeting with the handful of remaining parishioners, he was moved by one old man who asked to be excused from participating in the disposal, since he had belonged there since his boyhood.

Taking a Stand

As all sat in silence, Conwell asked them why they shouldn't start over again. Discussion led to a plan to get the church into shape for a service the next week. All agreed to meet the next morning, so Conwell scared up some tools, arrived at the church, and waited. Since no one came and the church was really beyond repair, he began tearing it down himself. A passerby asked him what he was doing. He replied he was going to build a new church. The fellow told Conwell that the people would never do that, but Conwell replied with certainty that they would.

The fellow told Conwell to stop by his livery stable that night and he would give him a hundred dollars for the church. Another man came along, and the same conversation ensued. When Conwell told him that the stable man was contributing, the other registered his disbelief, saying that he would match whatever the other gave—if in fact he gave anything at all.

The money, along with Conwell's irrepressible enthusiasm, energized the congregation to move forward. Conwell was ordained and hired as the new church's first pastor for $600 a year—quite a drop from his income as an attorney. Conwell arranged to have his salary doubled when the congregation doubled, which it did within the year.

This congregation healthy and growing, Conwell took another pay cut to help a failing church in Philadelphia. His new congregation began to grow by leaps and bounds also. They bought land and built a new church with a curious doorway on the second floor that Conwell laughed away as a good potential for a fire escape.

One day after Sunday service, a young man came up to Conwell to discuss his problem in working and wanting to study for the ministry. No college existed to help him, and he was at a loss as to how to do it himself. Conwell told him to come to his house one evening the next week. The young man asked if he could bring a friend. Conwell replied he could bring as many as he wished.

Seven young men arrived to learn the foundations of Latin. Within three weeks, they numbered forty. Soon several hundred were studying in two houses at night and anytime they needed, to allow for their ongoing employment. This group grew into what is today known as Temple University. The mysterious second-story door of Temple Church opens right into one of the main buildings.

At the time of this biography, Conwell was in his seventies. Over 80,000 students had attended the institution. Conwell also founded a local hospital and became president of a second, the whole time being the "most famous" lecturer of his day, often delivering over 200 lectures in different cities each year with no airplanes to speed his travels. He earned over $4,000,000 [$145,000,000 in 1993 money], the proceeds of which went to help young people working their way through college. Not a penny went to Conwell.

Courage, Perseverance, and Learning and Growing

Over the years, Conwell exhibited the courage necessary to live a life of purpose. He went out on financial limbs, often receiving needed money the day foreclosure proceedings were to begin. He faced rejection and derision by fellow Baptist ministers. His courage was contagious and encouraged many others to engage in his purpose fulfillment. We see here the power of commitment we discussed in the last chapter.

Perseverance characterized his daily life, from legendary war efforts saving his men to his singlehanded efforts to save a dying church. Sixteen hours of daily work, raising a family, and hundreds of speaking engagements annually only begin to indicate the perseverance of this man, who prepared two sermons weekly and thought nothing of going to a dying parishioner's bedside, something that would be uncommon in a parish minister with a congregation numbering in the thousands.

Through all this, Conwell was learning and growing constantly. His sermons and books gave testimony to his continual quest for self-improvement. Similarly, he added to the learning and growing of countless others through his teaching, preaching, friendship, and sterling example of expecting the best from himself and others. Conwell lived the phrase he was so fond of using: "All good things are possible."

He believed strongly in a loving God who wants the best for His children, and he believed our destiny is in our own hands. His purpose was to demonstrate this to all he met and invite them into the adventure of full loving existence, and he never seemed to forget it. Courage, perseverance, and learning and growing were daily realities Conwell lived that resulted in this inspiring example of a man of purpose.

Conwell represents to me the finest that can manifest in human beings. He learned and grew out of his love and service to others. He must rarely have found himself far from his purpose. It's easy to be intimidated or misled by his working sixteen hours for every workday. I think this perception is in error. What strikes me as most compelling about the man is his caring and his willingness to respond to any work set before him. This led him from book to book and from career to career early in his life, learning each step of the way.

Later on, tending to what was wanted and needed led him from a lucrative law career into the reconstruction and resuscitation of a church. Responding to the needs of this pastorless church, he became a pastor and ultimately the founder of a pioneering university and hospital. The whole time, he was speaking to some thirteen million people about how magnificent they were and how they could start right where they were to become all they could and wanted to be.

To be sure, his hours were impressive, but I suspect that more central was his focus on the sword that acted as a daily reminder of his higher purpose. I suspect too that the sword was secondary to what it symbolized to Conwell: that someone had died for love of him, so the least he could do was live fully his love for others.

There are those who believe that central to each of our purposes is not only learning, growing, and serving but learning to love fully. Most of these people will tell you love is the essential element to our being, and that as we live our lives purposefully, we align ourselves with that essential loving self. Living to our highest clears us for loving—it is as if our nonessential self is being burned away and our true self is emerging in the process. Focus on purpose helps us into and through this purification of love.

Our purpose statement should provide a verbal representation of that essential self. It gives us a tuning fork to which we can orient, just as Conwell oriented to the sword every morning. This tuning fork gives us a baseline to which we attune so that we can live our daily lives engaging in thoughts and actions as closely attuned to our highest self as possible. When we live ever closer attunement, we automatically begin to drop our lower self and live increasingly from our higher self. Conwell's sword helped him remember to do this, cutting away limitation and crafting a world of possibility.

Conwell was learning to love throughout his life. Every project he undertook was larger than the one before and stretched him further in love, trust, and his ability to inspire his fellow men to their highest. His purpose was being fulfilled as he learned. He saw himself learning to experience the love of God more fully and was engaged in helping others do the same. He did this in the biographies he wrote of great men, his legal work—where he only served in causes he saw as being "in the right"—his teaching, leading, and, ultimately, in his ministering.

So we see how living with full purpose increases productivity and efficiency not by technique but by engaging in the largest enterprise possible, one that draws the best out of us and draws the best to us—throughout our lifetime.

In our consideration of purpose, we have seen people learning to love more fully by living to their highest purpose. Like Conwell, they have demonstrated courage, persistence, and learning.

Courage was necessary for Marsha as she used higher purpose to guide her in letting go of clients as objects in sales and began serving fully. It took great courage for her to learn new ways of operating. She needed to persist, because her old habits died hard and her learning was slow.

Don Moon showed perseverance and courage as he led the resurrection of Shimer College. The lessons the college needed and needs to learn in following its dream are many and never-ending. Each success brings with it new challenges that require courage and perseverance along with learning and development.

It is his vision of a truly humanitarian educational system that keeps Don going. His purpose to educate students to be the most effective loving citizens possible animates this vision and draws him forward into his fullest potential as priest, educator, and, most of all, fellow traveler. Just as Conwell's sword reminded him of the love available to him, Don's students call him to his highest.

Ellis has a vision that emanates from his purpose. He sees a just society in which each individual is fully supported to live to his fullest. Business is the vehicle to this for him, and he dedicates himself to the most effective, rational, and humane business world possible. Every sales call is an opportunity to fulfill each of his missions, teaching him the skills he needs to succeed. It is only this dedication that keeps him going, like Conwell with the sword of his purpose, cutting away his barriers, living his life to its fullest in service, education, and, ultimately, love.

Ellis's dedication includes regular and consistent coaching. Learning is essential to him. He uses personal support and reflection to keep himself on track. He knows he is more courageous when focused and persistent using reminders from others and learns best when understanding and growing from what he is doing.

We all need help in purpose fulfillment. No matter how sharp our sword or how present we can keep it before us, we need covoyagers, cheerleaders, teachers, and many more to cut away the brambles and other barriers on our way to our highest. The journey is epic, with long distances and never-ending barriers to overcome. Each of us is Ulysses with sirens and rocks trying to stop us daily.

We all hesitate, and we all do stop. We need not only our commitments but the love and goodwill of others to help get ourselves back up and keep wielding the sword. In a beautiful recounting of her chance encounter with spectators at the twenty-fifth mile marker of a twenty-six-mile marathon, Laura Mayer talks of the cheering crowd that knew its mission with the latecomers. The winners had passed by well over an hour earlier. The crowd was not there to cheer on racers to a finish line but to encourage heroes who had staked themselves in a do-or-die stand to face personal dragons in the pursuit of their highest.

There was the father pushing his son's wheelchair through the sand who waved with blistered hands in response to cheers—the woman in a daze, stumbling for want of a shoelace, which spectators immediately jumped to provide, pulling replacements from their own shoes as they went—the child running beside his grandfather as two middle-aged sons bicycled next to their mother, leaning over to ask, "Mom, you okay?"

We all need each other if we are going to make it. Conwell needed the thousands who voyaged with him, and we each need all the help we can get, too. Courage, perseverance, and learning and growing start with us but require a complex partnership of coaching and a cheering section of our own. The more we keep our eyes fixed on our highest, the more readily we can receive the support we need.

Tell your purpose, share your purpose—keep it over your bed, like Conwell—but always remember that it is not a solitary adventure. If humanity is to reach its highest, our capacity to love in all we do, it will only be accomplished by each of us taking full responsibility and standing shoulder to shoulder in unity, especially at work.

> *Our deepest fear is not that we are inadequate, our deepest fear is that we are powerful beyond measure. You are a child of God. Your playing small does not serve the world. There's nothing enlightened about shrinking so that other people won't feel insecure around you. We were born to manifest the glory of God that is within us. And as we let our own light shine, we unconsciously give other people permission to do the same. As we are liberated from our own fear, our presence automatically liberates others.*
>
> ...MARIANNE WILLIAMSON

Part 2

Corporate Principles and Purpose

Chapter 9

Discovering Purpose in Organizations

When a company stops looking for the best way to serve and turns to lesser ways such as the cheapest, its soul begins to shrivel.

The corporate purpose statement acts like the tuning fork for a band. The tuning fork emits a tone to which the group tunes so it can play in harmony. Similarly, an effective corporate purpose statement provides a common point of reference so different functions can all act in harmony. Corporate purpose statements tend to be developed in one of two ways. In the first, corporate purpose is an extension of the founder or owner. In the second, a purpose statement is developed by employees, often all in a small corporation or, in larger corporations, generally by a group of key executives. Sadly, only rarely is a statement for a large corporation developed by the entire company. The co-development of the corporate statement encourages "ownership." In the worst cases, a communications expert or outside firm develops the statement for the corporation.

There are innumerable variations on these themes. Some owners develop their own and then include employees. In the case of partnerships, the statement can be developed as a group or created by each individual, then finally synthesized.

Regardless, each person involved in the development of a corporate purpose statement is best served by first developing his or her own personal statement. The corporate purpose statement might be viewed as an umbrella within which each individual purpose fits. The greater the participation in formulation and the more true the reflection, the more employees will take ownership in the statement.

CORPORATE PURPOSE

A corporate purpose statement may include numerous missions, such as community, investor, employee, customer, and societal.

Many corporations develop strong customer missions and ultimately end up weak in the area of personnel. Too often, fear-oriented emphasis on shareholder return precludes a full focus on the well-being of personnel and, in many cases, even the best for customers. How can companies expect the best when it is not reciprocated? We cannot say which mission statement beyond customer and personnel you should include in your corporate purpose, but we do point out the necessity that all missions you choose be balanced. Profit and organizational

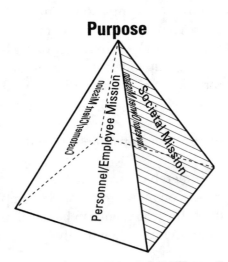

Figure 9.1

health provide accountability and must be included. The well-being of employees cannot exist without organizational well-being. Overemphasizing shareholder and customer missions at the expense of employee mission can lead to problems in the long run. It's like having a stool with one leg too short—precarious!

Unfortunately, many purpose statements are developed by some executive or outside firm designated by the president. Better not to bother at all—those statements will easily be perceived by employees as hypocritical and can rankle.

Some corporations do a two-to-five-day retreat for executives to develop a corporate purpose statement. This can be both inspiring and rewarding or frustrating and disillusioning. When there is true participation and genuine concern, the exercise can unify and inspire for years to come. When there is no follow-through or the statement does not fit with actual practice, the result is disheartening.

Purpose is a rarefied abstraction, difficult for corporations to apply in day-to-day transactions, except for the most adept. Just as it is for individuals. Many break down and give up. Because purpose is difficult to live and requires a high level of skill to implement effectively, we will discuss corporate principles and various plans to implement corporate purpose statements later. The principles of corporate purpose give accessible sets of more concrete indicators that can provide more immediate guidance in every choice, utterance, and interaction. The vehicles presented here will show ways to apply these in planning, visioning, and performance enhancement.

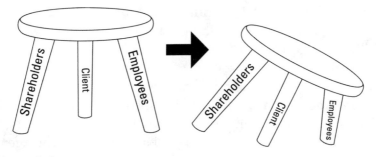

Figure 9.2

LIMITED PURPOSE STATEMENTS

Too many purpose statements are simply inadequate. In the mid-eighties, one of the big eight accounting firms in Chicago had one such statement, developed at a very expensive two-day off-site partners' retreat. It was posted near elevators and meeting rooms throughout the company. The stated purpose was long and ponderous, but the essence was to be the second biggest accounting firm.

A host of other good ideas could not disguise that the purpose was to be number two. Not only did this fail the never-ending, ever-expanding test, but it was not reciprocal, failed to include its various missions, and most sadly, failed to inspire most people in the firm. High-level employees and partners who attended the retreat spoke of the statement with disdain and derision as the office head's mission, or his "baby."

In general, developing a corporate purpose statement follows the same process as an individual statement. We'll now follow three corporations as they develop their statements: a sole ownership, a family-owned partnership, and a wholly-owned division of a parent company.

We read about Ed earlier. He was hired to head the South American branch of a multinational bank with staff from numerous countries. We'll call it Interbank. The corporation had not grown significantly in the twenty years since it had been acquired by its parent company. Recent consulting reports from Peat Marwick and McKinsey focused on marketing failures and the conflict among departments and cultures. No consultant's advice had been heeded prior to Ed's arrival.

The predominately South American service staff was at odds with the European sales and business development staff. Neither was functioning particularly well, new sales were minuscule, and the organization regularly sent out error-ridden statements to depositors more than two weeks late.

In order to unify the staff, Ed spent his first two months learning about the bank and then took the four directors on retreat to review problems and strengths of the bank. They generated a purpose statement and then developed a common vision of their ideal state. An exhaustive list of possible strategies to move from their present state toward their ideal was then created.

Central to the common vision they held was the exercise in developing their corporate purpose statement and the principles of operation that we will review later. Before they even began looking at current problems and strengths, pathways or vision, they focused on why they were there, arriving at the following purpose statement:

> To engage fully and professionally in the creation of financial success for all our constituencies:
> - to provide wealth enhancement and security for clients;
> - financial security and personal growth for our employees;
> - and exceptional returns on both financial and human capital employed for the shareholders.

The three legs of their stool were strongly outlined. We see here distinct mission statements for staff, clients, and shareholders. With this perspective, they began fleshing out their vision and ways to accomplish it. They continued by identifying the principles of purpose and operating agreements to realize these principles. We will see some of the ways they operationalized these in Chapter 10.

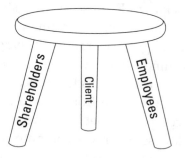

Figure 9.3

With this done, a context of agreement, safety, and alignment had been established—allowing for a swift, painless airing of the long-standing differences that had concerned the consultants. The result was astonishing to all. With a clear statement of purpose, differences could be resolved more easily by calling each party to the highest manifestation of the vision. Solid purpose statements clarify turf and personality conflict when used objectively. Many of the petty executive-suite and back-room conflicts that drag companies down shrivel when exposed in good faith to the light of a true statement of the universal good.

The hard-driving, Euro-Germanic business development staff felt appreciated for their role while understanding for the first time how their abrupt manner could be divisive in the culture of the bank. Likewise, the Hispanic service staff began to recognize the valid frustration of the business development staff when their concern for the relationship and operations side of the business was valued.

The new shared vision flowing from the corporate purpose statement provided the foundation for a restructuring—helping the bank reduce other interdepartmental and intercultural friction. Functional departments were dissolved and crossfunctional service teams developed to integrate service and sales, provide more personal service, and, ultimately, to develop a more effective sales effort from the inside out.

PARTNERS

Carmine and Mack own Readiserve Drugstores Inc., a chain of twelve full-service drugstores. Carmine is president and Mack vice president in charge of operations. Their grandfather started the business; Carmine's father was the former president. Before Mack became vice president, his father occupied his position.

Carmine built the chain from two to twelve stores shortly after joining the company. I met him when he called to ask me to present a one-day seminar on communications to his staff. When I asked him why he wanted a seminar on communications, he listed a number of problems that really represented a deeper lack of corporate alignment and cooperation.

He was surprised when I declined to do the seminar, saying that I saw no reason to get the staff all excited only to have their hopes dashed because no one was practicing what I was preaching. Not only would they "unlearn" any positive lessons fast, they would become hardened toward future learning because of this disillusionment.

Carmine asked what I proposed. I said that the best thing I could think of would be for him to become a walking communications seminar—any substantial change needed to start with him.

He then brought Mack in to talk with me further and explore this direction. We discussed living a life of purpose and reinvesting the enterprise with a clear purpose. Our conversation was easy, since they both already felt clear spiritual focus and purpose in their personal lives. They had simply never attempted to apply this focus at work. They were excited by the possibility of having a similar, unified clarity in business.

Mack was a devout Christian, whose personal purpose revolved around his developing ability to love and grow in his relationship to Christ. He saw family, work, community, and personal missions for himself. He was excited to articulate them and consider the possibility of integrating his work, church, and family lives.

Carmine's life purpose statement was concerned with spiritual but not specifically Christian issues. Learning, personal growth, and the development of consciousness were most critical to him. Carmine ran a small, private publishing company on the side that brought spiritual teachings from other cultures and religions to the United States market. Carmine's mission included the whole human community and the town they lived in, where he was school board president.

Once the two of them had developed their personal statements, they were ready to develop the purpose statement for their chain. Strangely, after several meetings, they still could not settle on a statement so we could proceed. They could state that their mission in service to serve their employees, communities, families, and selves both for profit and the betterment of all, but the words kept changing, and no substantial progress was being made.

Finally, they revealed being afraid to present any of the statements to their fellow owners and directors—namely, their parents. A deep ideological and stylistic rift between the generations became obvious—it is fairly common for purpose statement development to bring such disconnections to light.

Carmine and Mack knew their parents had a different mission for the company. Their mission development was stalled because it did not reflect the intent of the "powers that be" in the corporation. They were surprised at the magnitude of the invisible wall into which they were repeatedly bumping. Finally, they resolved to discuss the problem with their parents, who joined them in reducing the conflict, gladly selling the chain wholly to the two. Developing a corporate statement commonly uncovers differences in values and even uncovers cases of people operating at cross purposes. In Carmine and Mack's case, the situation was resolved when the younger generation purchased the corporation with the surprise blessing of their elders.

SOLE OWNERSHIP

Mike Zwell owns and runs Zwell International, an executive search firm dedicated to bringing the best of social science to bear in executive searches, in order to assure the brightest futures for the individuals placed, their families, and the firms that hire them.

Mike developed a purpose statement of his own and then refined it with his staff to be sure it reflected their will and sense of purpose. They spent a great deal of time identifying and refining the principles of purpose for themselves.

The purpose of their company, as they see it, is "To facilitate our clients, employees, their families, others whom we serve, and the society at large in realizing their true, most magnificent, capable, loving selves through the performance of executive search and related human resource activities, and to have a profitable enterprise thereby. To fully embody the principles we are committed to, and to expand the adherence to these principles through company growth."

It's important to note that they include profit in their statement. Sometimes this is overly emphasized as an end in itself and in others, especially service firms, it is forgotten, reflecting the company's failure to focus on this level of fiscal accountability.

Many corporations are beginning to expand their definitions of the bottom line as they develop a clear sense of higher purpose. For them, profit begins with dollars and cents but expands to include human capital, family well-being, and the benefit of the larger society.

In the case of Mike's company, we see a mission statement flexible enough to handle a full range of contingencies, with profit defined as a by-product of purpose. This interesting perspective acknowledges the importance of profit while clearly demonstrating the company's assumption that profit is a by-product of service.

MOVING ON

We now move on to corporate purpose implementation practices, especially the principles of corporate purpose. We will discuss several ways to leverage, enhance, and empower performance with purpose through development and use of the corporate principles.

Chapter 10

Corporate Principles and Tools for Application

This section introduces you to some ways corporations that have developed their own principles of purpose implement them. This should help you apply your own creativity and values in developing principles and methods of applications that are appropriate to you, your company, culture, values, purpose, and vision. The corporate principles of purpose work as core pillars of your company's success strategy. They represent the essence of what you believe is necessary to the success and fulfillment of your purpose. They turn that purpose into dynamic tools useful in daily operations.

All businesses operate from principles, whether we know it or not. Principles are at the root of all our actions, operating on an unconscious level most of the time and directing our thoughts, reactions, and plans. If we operate from a principle such as economy, we concern ourselves with things such as maximizing, minimizing, motivating, punishing, and so on. Operating from a principle such as accountability we might focus on things such as deadlines, quotas, controls, or costs. We identify two types of principles, those of abundance and those of regression or scarcity. Principles of abundance tend to be creative whereas principles of scarcity tend to be reactive. If we do not articulate the principles of our higher purpose and make a point of living by them consciously, we are more likely to allow our actions to be guided by unconscious, limiting, regressive principles. Regressive principles are based on limitation. In regressive principles, we see reactivity as opposed to creativity, overcontrol as opposed to cooperation, and limitation as opposed to maximization. They tend to lead to less creative, less satisfying outcomes.

I experienced the problems of regressive principles in growing my first company, Human Effectiveness, with my partner, Bob Kauffman. We had our first major personnel crisis in our ninth year of business. We had been growing at rates of twenty to thirty percent for a number of years and had begun hiring and promoting staff out of the heavy demands of growing service needs. We were confused between delivering enough service and sticking true to our standards. In hindsight, it is easy to see that we should have been willing to forgo certain business and grow more slowly. Instead, we chose to force the issue and paid a steep price in exchange for some valuable lessons.

We already knew that it generally took us four years to bring a staff member of Ph.D. level with over ten years behind him or her up to speed. The new staff we hired from the pressure of extreme need lacked either qualities or experience we wanted. On top of that, we moved them too quickly. We let principles of scarcity determine our actions and had people engaged in service delivery beyond their abilities and/or maturity.

We were asking people to perform at a level they couldn't deliver. The results were disastrous. We hadn't yet developed the training, quality assurance, and quality control measures we needed to assure our standards. We couldn't maintain our desired levels of excellence in service. We lost clients and staff as never before. Even though we ultimately learned to train faster, monitor quality better, and train clients to use the service more effectively, the lessons took years to implement and clearly pointed out how our failure to stay true to our higher principles resulted in problems.

Our fear of losing potential clients had driven us more strongly than our focus on quality and our capacity to deliver the best. We lacked maturity and skill. We had never made mistakes at this level before, so we clearly had a lot to learn. The principles of purpose were useful to us as we analyzed the problems and made adjustments—ultimately leading to improvements all around. This is, in fact, one of the functions of principles of purpose: to give us a touchstone or measuring stick by which we can assess errors, learn the lessons and be stronger, better businesspeople, and more effective citizens.

Top sports teams analyze every game, looking to see where they are failing to implement their strategy and adjusting course accordingly. Players and playing units are graded according to the effectiveness of their execution of the game plan. The game plan is the application of the team's chosen principles in the game itself. Whether consciously or unconsciously, teams use their principles of operation to determine their strategies.

Consciously chosen principles of organizational purpose give a consistent, coherent foundation from which to examine our performance and toward which we can direct our future actions. The Chicago Bulls, three-time world basketball champions, based their success on principles such as selfless play, flow, allowing the hottest hand to express himself fully, and flexibility. They chose a strategy appropriate to these principles, the triangle offense. This offense allows them to evolve an attack from a basic structure. The structure is simple and straightforward, allowing the greatest creativity but demanding absolute adherence to their principles, including selflessness and flow. It is intended to facilitate the greatest offensive expression available on any given evening and requires precise coordinated effort.

Boiling the game down to its essential principles and training the team to implement them is the genius of the Bulls' coach, Phil Jackson. He lives true to his principles as consistently as possible in practices, meetings, and games. He influences his men in as many ways as possible through suggested reading and mind-sharpening activities. The team displays strong symbols on the walls of their locker and meeting rooms to remind them of their higher orientation and inspire them to their best.

Just as the world champion Bulls must keep learning the principles essential to their success, so must we. Learning principles of purpose is a lifelong endeavor—we grow, situations change, our products evolve, and personnel shift. When we have clearly articulated principles and purpose statements, they help us adapt and grow. Phil Jackson has spent his life developing the principles that guide the Bulls. This process is described in his inspiring book, *Sacred Hoops*.

Now that we have looked at how individuals develop principles of purpose, let's look at three companies as examples of how corporate purpose is articulated and implemented. Whereas the individual principles of purpose are standard and follow human development to responsibility and higher purpose, the corporate principles have more variation. They provide more of a game plan or guide to purpose fulfillment and will ultimately be more likely to succeed when implemented by people practicing the personal principles of purpose fulfillment.

ZWELL INTERNATIONAL

> *We assume that each of us is responsible for our own success, that we are authors of our own reality. We are not victims. At every moment we have complete freedom of choice.*
>
> ...ZWELL INTERNATIONAL

We already read about Zwell International's purpose statement development. Mike, the sole owner of the corporation, developed the statement and then had his staff make it theirs in a workshop, where they reworded it to include and reflect their perspective.

They came up with the following statement: "To facilitate our employees, their families, those we serve, and the society at large in the realization of our true, most magnificent potential selves through the performance of executive search and related human resource activities and to have a profitable enterprise thereby; to fully embody the principles we are committed to and to expand the adherence to these principles through personal and company growth."

In the exercise to identify their key principles they first identified and defined the following twenty-two principles they considered important for the success and fulfillment of their company's purpose. These principles were combined and refined after the creative session in which they were developed. In it no ideas were discounted or rejected and everyone was strongly encouraged to participate and risk:

Accountability. We agree to be held to our word, to be expected and held accountable to keep our explicit and implicit agreements and to accept appropriate consequences for failure. Consequences are to be structured as educational and self-development opportunities.

Commitment. To engage fully to fulfill our declarations, to apply ourselves as completely as possible until completion. We assume that this is necessary to the greatest fulfillment of our purpose as well as personal fulfillment.

Excellence. We commit to the highest level of quality in every aspect of our work to assure the best possible results for our clients. We assume that this is a key to the greatest pride and personal fulfillment available to us.

Fiscal responsibility. Invest and manage resources wisely; plan for droughts; set and meet fiscal goals and standards. We assume that this is critical for the optimum deployment of our resources.

Focus. Apply full attention to the task at hand; commit fully to successful completion of that task. We assume that this level of attentiveness will enhance performance and ultimately our purpose fulfillment.

Play. Engage fully, work hard with a playful attitude, and make our work satisfying and nourishing. We assume that we perform and learn better with full engagement in the here and now in a way that causes us to grow and be nourished by our work.

Respect. See and expect the best from each other; acknowledge the importance of diversity in opinion; acknowledge the validity of each others' opinions

Responsibility. Take ownership of the results around us and see ourselves as the creators of our own realities; avoid blame and deliver solutions without complaints and criticisms. We assume that this level of personal responsibility is necessary for the greatest fulfillment of our various missions.

Teamwork. Value each other; commit to each other's success; act with goodwill towards each other; support common goals, principles, and standards; accept each other; hold each other to the highest standards.

Truth. Express the truth as fully as possible for the fulfillment of our common purpose; speak personally for ourselves, risk displeasing others for the well-being of the company by telling the hard truths. We assume that the fullest expression of truth will lead to the most complete sharing of information necessary to the fulfillment of our various missions.

Winning. As distinct from 'doing our best.' We play to win.

Aliveness. Be fully present with our thoughts, feelings, energy and body in the service of the company's purpose.

Completion. Abandon no interaction or project until it is complete, which means finished to company standards, consciously tabled, or consciously and purposefully dropped.

Do our best. Apply full power, energy, and intent to the task at hand and take responsibility and coaching in the down times.

Full expression. Express fully all thoughts and feelings relating to the delivery of the finest product possible and the fulfillment of the company purpose. We assume that full expression will lead to full engagement and the best application of our capacities to the success of our mission.

Good faith. Operate in accordance with both stated and implied agreements to deliver the best for ourselves and others; acknowledge and clear unfinished business by fully discussing limiting thoughts and feelings such as envy and competition.

Here and now. Live and experience fully in the present. We assume that our most powerful expression and therefore likelihood of success comes with no baggage from the past or undue fears about the future. To this end we keep ourselves current and up-to-date so we can be fully focused on our purpose.

Intentionality. Acknowledge goals and state our intention to achieve them. We assume that intention governs all that we do and therefore intend to analyze and change misdirected intention in problems and develop increasingly powerful intentions toward our purpose fulfillment.

Patience. Strive to achieve the serenity to accept what cannot be changed, the courage to change what can be, and the wisdom to know the difference.

Service. Provide desired and needed services to our clients, coworkers, selves, the company, our families, and our communities. We assume that service is the best way to personal satisfaction and the realization and fulfillment of our purposes.

Speak only for self. We assume that confusion and irresponsibility abound in situations of gossip and irresponsible communication. We therefore strive to communicate responsibly by speaking only for ourselves and avoiding gossip and irresponsible generalizations.

Stand up for self. We assume that each of us is ultimately responsible for our own satisfaction and success. Furthermore, we assume that the success of the company rests on the success of each individual. To that end, we support a culture in which each person has the right and responsibility to stand up for themselves within the scope of the purpose of the company.

Combining and Focusing

They then discussed and reviewed these principles to arrive at the four key principles by which they would conduct their business. They considered these to be a complete and manageable set of principles which, enacted in strategy, should lead to success. To arrive at these four, they combined redundant principles where possible, looked for more powerful ones that subsumed others, and affirmed the importance of but dropped from the list those they found less compelling.

Zwell International Operating Principles

A set of four principles guide our company in the fulfillment of its purpose. They are:

Responsibility • Commitment • Service • Play

Principle One: Responsibility

We assume that each of us is fully responsible for our own and the company's satisfaction and fulfillment, that our purpose fulfillment is totally in our own hands; that we are responsible to generate and employ the resources necessary for client satisfaction, our own success, and ultimately the fulfillment of the company purpose.

We assume that each of us is responsible for our own success, that we are authors of our own reality. We are not victims. At every moment we have complete freedom of choice to act in any way that does not defy the laws of nature. Any beliefs or attitudes implying that we do not have this freedom result from limiting past experiences and misinformation that keeps us from taking full and total charge of our lives.

In every moment we have a choice of accepting responsibility or blaming others for it. When we take the position that others are to blame and that we are passive victims, we limit our possibilities of success in sales, service, and team performance. We tend to adopt attitudes of hopelessness and stagnancy that limit our production and satisfaction. We recognize that we have a lot of power to change ourselves and very little to change others. When we take responsibility, when we choose to focus on our contribution to the current state of affairs, then we can more readily change ourselves to make our reality how we want it.

When we take responsibility we use resources better and arrive at more creative solutions for the problems that face us. Our clients are better served and we maximize the successful fulfillment of our mission. Practically, the principle of responsibility actualizes itself through our work in these ways:

- we communicate fully our thoughts and feelings on a project
- we each take 100 percent responsibility for the outcome of a shared project
- we bring out the best in each other through challenge and support
- we succeed, celebrating our victories, and seek to learn how to reproduce and improve on them
- when something we do fails to meet expectations, we look and learn from the situation so that we can do better the next time.
- when we have a conflict, we seek to resolve it with responsible communication, acknowledging our role and learning from it so that we can have the most harmonious, productive relationships possible
- understanding that we create our own satisfaction, we take on the challenge of making our professional lives deeply satisfying and meaningful

Principle Two: Commitment

We not only declare goals which will help us fulfill our purpose, but we apply ourselves fully to that end. We dedicate our best selves to that end with unwavering dedication until the task is completed. We apply ourselves fully in the here and now with full intention, expression, aliveness, and accountability.

Commitment involves putting our best, our whole being, into what we do. As we set goals and strive to achieve our purposes, we don't hold back. We believe that it is by choosing stretch goals that we will learn, grow, and fulfill our purpose to its fullest. Fulfillment and satisfaction are not possible without commitment. We know this because we undertake and thrive on tasks that leave us challenged and somewhat uncertain, bringing out our best. People who run races without goals are less likely to put forth full effort. Without worthy competition they tend not to experience the full satisfaction of their best run. Commitment evidences itself at Zwell International in these ways:

- hard work, we put forth energy and effort to get the job done
- we know and support each other's goals
- we focus our attention on the immediate task at hand
- we keep each other informed of goal progress and solicit the best talent and help of the firm in our dedication to bringing the best possible service to our client
- winning is a constant focus for individuals, teams, and clients

Principle Three: Service

Service is the principle by which we act to help others achieve their higher purposes. At its highest level, our primary interest is to act on our best thinking and to bring to bear our greatest resources in the best interest of others.

We are committed to serving our customers and candidates to the best of our abilities. We are committed to keeping the business focused on the highest service in technology and quality that we can attain in response to their needs.

The highest quality relationships in our business are those in which our clients and candidates know that we care about them and their best interests. We assume that the higher the level of service we provide, the stronger our business will be. There is no higher principle than that of service. By committing our lives to service, we dedicate ourselves to serving the greater good and to having others truly benefit by our contact with them, whether they engage our professional services or not.

We assume that service is all we do. Every activity in which we engage, including sales, should lead to a net gain for our clients and prospective clients. We also assume that every interaction between us internally is an opportunity to serve each other and thereby our clients. We assume that we must experience service to give it maximally and that in its highest form, service generates and nourishes—instead of draining—leading to a creative, synergistic process.

Our vision of service includes:

- going the extra mile to satisfy clients' and each others needs
- asking ourselves regularly how we can better serve and be served, developing the company to its highest
- identifying and correcting problems as quickly as possible
- asking our customers to evaluate the quality of our service

- evaluating the quality and quantity of our service to each other
- including every other qualitative and quantitative aspect of our business in our evolving vision of service

Principle Four: Play

Play is the principle that most enhances our performance. We assume that we learn and perform at our best when playing full out. Play defines the nature of our moment-by-moment interactions with the world around us. Through play we are nourished and nurtured in what we do. We assume that play will lead to maximum satisfaction and appreciation.

When work is not play it is burden. Burden is a victim position. In burden we *have* to come to work rather than wanting to. In burden we feel unappreciated and operate in ways that will guarantee little appreciation. We know of people who have overcome extremes of victimhood and burden even flourishing in concentration camps. With this in mind, we apply ourselves to the fullest conscious, joyous engagement in our work. Together we can learn to make the load light.

Inherent in play for us is the concept of choice. We work here because it is what we choose. We are individually responsible for attaining our desired satisfaction and emotional fulfillment on the job. In this context we define work as "play for pay." We risk, try things, experiment and do things differently to learn, grow, and fulfill our purpose. The hours may be long, the work may be difficult, it may sometimes be painful, it may be frustrating, but it is all part of the "game" we are choosing to play. Play manifests itself at Zwell International by:

- finding ways to make work satisfying
- finding new, creative ways to serve clients

- finding the humor in what we do
- being able to make fun of ourselves
- playing full out
- risking
- interacting fully with each other
- keeping enjoyment before us as a desirable state
- taking individual responsibility for and committing ourselves to fulfillment and satisfaction
- stretching ourselves to learn and grow
- engaging fully to accomplish our goals

READISERVE DRUGSTORES

The Readiserve group chose seven principles of purpose that their owners, Carmine and Mack, spent two years learning to use before introducing them to their firm. They chose to introduce the principles to the firm managers through one of their quarterly evaluation and feedback meetings with store managers. The seven principles they chose were operationalized on a seven-point questionnaire about store operations. All employees in the chain filled out the forms for their managers. In addition, fellow managers and the owners filled out forms evaluating each manager. Carmine and Mack were evaluated by store managers, their direct reports, and each other.

Results were tabulated on a social science statistical package giving range, median, mean, distribution, and other statistics for the group, but what was most compelling about the process was the fact that Carmine and Mack made their personal feedback public first. This added a great deal of credibility to the program, especially since their scores in several categories were far from the top of the management group.

We will first see the five principles initially introduced to the employees in general; then we will see excerpts from a sample feedback form received by each manager prior to this general introduction. The first principle will be presented in its entirety; subsequent principles are abbreviated to save space. The feedback form is from one of the top managers in the firm. Feedback from some of the lower-performing managers would be too lengthy to reproduce here.

Introductory Document (presenting principles to the staff two years after the management survey)

Values & Principles

The following values and principles have been developed by Carmine and me, as the owners and managers of Readiserve, over the past several years. We have used them for some time and intend to continue using these values and principles to guide us in our decisions and actions. We hope that all of you, as members of the Readiserve Team, consider these values and principles appropriate and use them as a guide in your decisions and actions. We will all be learning to use them more effectively over time. If you feel that we need to add or delete any of these, please let us know. If we fail to live up to these, let us know. We consider the opportunity to work in a principled business a blessing and need your partnership for the highest fulfillment of all of our potential.

ACCOUNTABILITY refers to full responsibility for the consequences of our actions and for the success of the total enterprise.

EXCELLENCE is doing our best and learning to do better than our competition.
COMMITMENT is declaring results and accomplishing them.

INITIATIVE is not waiting for others to measure us—we measure ourselves.

MOTIVATION is keeping ourselves performing fully and supporting each other in this process.

NOURISHMENT is what we need for sustenance, growth, and thriving.

OPPORTUNITY is providing the possibility of developing ourselves fully.

EMPOWERMENT is encouraging development of our capabilities and talents and their creative application.

BALANCE is maintaining each aspect of our lives in appropriate proportion.

ABUNDANCE is knowing that life is providing us with the opportunities we need to meet our needs.

TRUST is living according to these principles and not basing our intentions and actions on fear.

GOOD FAITH is intending that our actions will result in what is best for all.

INCLUSION is considering how our actions affect ourselves and others.

CARING is relating to others with inclusion and respect.

RESPONSIBILITY is acting so that another need not doubt our word or commitment.

ALIVENESS is expressing our vitality in the present.

PLAY is enjoying what we do.

INITIATIVE is acting for the greater good and not just reacting to minimize problems.

LEARNING is identifying the lessons in our experiences and then applying these lessons to our lives.

CONSCIOUSNESS is performing our actions with full awareness and intent.

OPENNESS is relating to situations and others without preconditions or prejudice.

HONESTY is relating to ourselves and others without deception.

SHARING is providing others with access to our resources, experiences, lessons, and information.

COMMUNICATION is transferring information, thoughts, and feelings so that another can understand.

COOPERATION is interacting with others so that the combined efforts are beneficial to all involved.

Thank you for your partnership,

Mack
September 14, 1994

The Store Manager Feedback Form begins with the overall score, proceeds to the highest score, and arranges the rest in descending order.

Manager Feedback and Development Plan

Introduction

NAME, for the survey as a whole, you received an average score of 4.08 compared to the average for the whole Readiserve Group, which was 3.94. This means that employees and fellow managers agree that you exhibit these principles well, and on average do so to a slightly greater degree than the average manager in the chain.

The overall score is broken down into seven aspects or principles of the work environment: service, workability, accountability, nourishment, trust, aliveness, and openness. This section contains what we found significant in the surveys completed by your office staff and managers.

Each principle presents you first with statistical and verbal feedback, followed by a definition of the area measured, interpretation of the feedback, and a recommended course of action to correct any weaknesses.

The order of the principles listed below is based on the composite perception of your utilization of these principles in the company, starting with the highest score. Keep in mind that the scores given for each principle are averages, with a minimum score of 1.00 and maximum of 5.00. (For a breakdown of your scores for each individual question, see the table at the back of this report.)

1. ACCOUNTABILITY

A. *Results.* Your score for this principle is 4.49, compared to 4.16 for the Readiserve Group as a whole. Accountability is also the highest principle for the stores as a whole. In your self-assessment, you rated yourself at 4.00. Employee comments include the following:

"I believe he puts a lot of time and energy in self-improvement."
"He will also accept blame/praise for my area, which is a nice thing."

B. *Definition.* Accountability refers to full responsibility for the consequences of our actions and for the success of the total enterprise. Accountability includes *commitment* to the company's vision of *excellence* by the application of one's efforts and energies with dedication and alignment to principles such as those described here. It means taking *initiative* in responsibility for the overall results of the company. It rests upon self-accountability, *motivation* to be our best, and on the empowering of all employees to perform fully in their individual areas. This principle is reflected in survey statements such as:

"My manager wants our store to be the best we can be."
"My manager takes full responsibility for the consequences of his actions."

Accountability really means being "count-on-able" and includes reliability, willingness to take full responsibility for results, whatever they may be, and the continual alignment of employee efforts to the company vision. When it is present, employees feel part of a whole, are confident of their part in the larger picture, and more readily own their piece with pride.

Now there is an opportunity for you to discuss your personal philosophy. What is your understanding of accountability?

_____

_____

_____

_____

C. *Interpretation and Recommendations.* This is your highest area as measured by the assessment. You have clearly set the standard for the company in the area of accountability. We recommend that you recognize the importance of your skill in this area and learn to replicate yourself and assist all your direct reports in focusing on identifying and learning the skills they need to have their stores and areas be the best they can be. To the extent that they are trained to be fully accountable for the consequences of their actions, they can encourage accountability among each other and their employees.

Your managers and staff express great respect for your intention to be the best that you can be. Ask yourself how you can bring peers and reports in the rest of the chain up to your level of expectation? Your scores reflect a deep personal commitment to the success of the Readiserve Group. There is a significant positive gap between your self-assessment and that of your staff and managers. This can be seen as a reflection of your high expectations, intentions to be honest in completing the questionnaire, a recognition of your leadership, and desire to excel.

Specifically, your employees rated you very high in wanting your stores to be the best they can be. They felt that you do an excellent job of taking responsibility for the consequences of your actions through others. You hold them accountable for their areas and they appreciate this, along with you personally taking full responsibility to be the best you can be.

Accountability is "where the buck stops." In order for you to continue developing your strength as you forge into new areas, we recommend you discuss thoroughly the results of this assessment with your supervisor managers and employees and continue to clarify and develop your vision for them.

The one area of weakness for you in the realm of accountability is in communications. People do not feel fully informed by you and they are not always sure you want to hear what they have to say. "I find out late about things I should have known sooner . . . " "He rushes too much. . . . I know he cares but I don't feel I get his full attention. . . . It's too hard to get him to listen. . . . He's OK when you finally corner him." You need to be more aware of others' needs for information, and you could provide more open channels to receive information. Remember, accountability exists in human relations as well as results!

Accountability areas where I can congratulate myself:

_____

_____

_____

_____

Accountability areas in which I see a need for improvement:

_____

_____

_____

_____

My highest priority in the area of accountability is:

_____

_____

_____

_____

2. SERVICE

A. *Results.* Your score for the principle of service is 4.42, compared to 4.14 for the Readiserve Group. Your self-assessment was 4.00. Managers and staff offered these comments, which positively reflected this principle in the management of your area:

"Customers are always first and foremost."

"All of NAME's actions are taken with our customers' needs in mind."

They also expressed concerns about your commitment to their service as represented by the following:

"I very rarely see NAME in my department or at my store. When he does come out, he never leaves without criticizing or finding fault with something. This leaves us with a negative feeling. We need NAME to reassure us that we are doing a good job. That point aside, I feel very good about working with NAME."

B. *Definition.* Manager and staff perception of service in your area included their sense of your reliability, helpfulness, appropriateness, and professionalism. *Service* is meeting the needs of others. *Reliability* is doing what we say we will do, while *helpfulness* refers to the action of assisting others. Responding to a given situation in the best and most fitting way available defines *appropriateness*. *Professionalism* results when we *conduct* ourselves reliably in a way that provides consistent, predictable results and inspires confidence. Service to our customers, managers, and staff is reflected in survey statements such as

"My manager places a high priority on serving the needs of our customers."

"My manager is helpful when I need assistance."

C. *Interpretation and Recommendations.* (Mostly congratulatory.) Once again your weaker area shows up in the realm of human relations and communication. Your staff needs to experience being fully served by you if you expect them to serve others fully. This means taking more time to hear their concerns. You seem to meet their needs in equipment, skill training, and other areas but fall short in relationships.

3. ALIVENESS

A. *Results*. Your score for the area of aliveness is 4.18, compared to 3.94 for the Readiserve Group overall. Your self-assessment was 3.66. Employee comments reflect both positive and negative experience among employees in this area. Some employees state:

"When he takes time to think about his actions, his enthusiasm usually gets anticipated results."

"He has taught me to engage actively in solving problems and acting spontaneously to serve."

Others express concern about the negativity they feel:

"When he comes into my area, he says nice things but right before he goes he always has something bad to say, and that's what the employee remembers."

"Atmosphere is stifled. Small talk is crushed almost immediately."

B. *Definition*. We see aliveness as vital to satisfaction and success. Aliveness is reflected in an attitude of playing the game, creating the atmosphere, taking the initiative, eagerness to learn, and general consciousness. *Aliveness* manifests when we live and work expressing our full vitality in the present. *Play* means that we enjoy what we do and engage fully in our work activities. *Initiative* results when play translates into concern for excellence and the good of all involved. People act to create the positive instead of reacting to avoid the negative. *Learning* results when we take in and apply new information and by turning it into usable skills. *Consciousness* results as we strive to perform with positive intentions and full awareness. This is reflected in survey statements such as:

"My manager maintains a positive store atmosphere."
"My manager encourages me to learn from my experiences."

When fully alive, a person is conscious of his surroundings, the quality of interactions with others, and his own intentions in the moment. He is continually, responsibly self-expressed, not "hanging on to something." Employees feel his presence as an encouragement, a giving, and a source of their own energy.

4. WORKABILITY

A. *Results.* Your score for this area is 4.08, compared to 3.98 for the entire Readiserve Group. Your self-assessment was 3.25. Employee comments include these:

"We are support for the stores, which fits with overall vision."
"There are many 'unwritten rules' that were set years ago that we continue to live by. I would like to see this company reevaluate company policy on things that could improve our quality of life in the workplace."
"He expects me to know automatically how to do a new duty. Sometimes I feel inadequate because I don't know."

B. *Workability.* This area was assessed by getting feedback on the perceived value placed on appropriate utilization of employee abilities, simplicity of procedures, convenience of operations to employees and customers, and integration of all functions in the store. *Workability* is assuring that a given task or system is possible, doable, and appropriate. *Simplicity* operates by accomplishing goals with minimum effort and expense of time, personnel and other resources. *Conve-*

nience is simplicity in service to customers and *integration* assures that all activities relate and function in harmony with the store's overall vision.

This principle is suggested in the survey by the following:

"My manager does not unnecessarily complicate tasks in my store."

"My manager makes sure that I have what I need to do my job well."

5. NOURISHMENT

A. *Results.* Your score for this principle is 3.71, compared to 3.72 for the combined Readiserve stores. Your self-assessment was 3.66. Employees offered the following positive comments:

"I enjoy what I do and learn something new each day."

"I feel NAME encourages me to make decision on my own. He often asks, "How do you feel about this?"

"I believe he sees untapped talents in me, and he is determined to help me bring them out."

The following negative assessments were also given:

"Not enough positive recognition reinforcement. Mistakes are always brought up, sometimes overdramatically, with terms like 'horrible' and 'awful,' etc."

"My life appears to be of no concern to my manager."

"He's preoccupied and unhappy too much."

B. *Definition.* The level of nourishment in the company was measured by assessing your employees' sense of opportunity, empowerment, balance, and abundance at work. Nourishment is what the environment provides for sustenance and personal growth. When we are nourished we are *empowered* to develop our capabilities and talents. We have the *opportunity* to apply our personal resources creatively. A *balanced* life allows us to grow as we fully assimilate our nourishment. When we feel fully nourished, an attitude of *abundance* prevails in all we do and we nourish those around us. This principle is reflected in such survey statements as:

"My job is a positive influence in my life."

"My manager is willing to make a tough decision even if it is unpopular."

C. *Interpretation and Recommendations.* The entire company is weaker here. Although you rate at average, you could probably enjoy your work more and your employees express satisfaction in many ways but indicate hunger in others. You seem to hold things as a burden and operate as a lone ranger where you could clearly benefit from more spontaneous contact and learning to enjoy your interactions more. Your staff was most divided on this point. Perhaps there is some favoritism working against you in this area too. The counselors at the employee assistance program or seminars on teamwork and creativity might be able to help you improve in this area.

6. TRUST

A. *Results.* Your score for this principle is 3.68, compared to 3.80 for all stores in the Readiserve Group. Your self-assessment was 3.41. Your employees' comments include the following:

"My suggestions for better ways to do things are often listened to and acted on by NAME."

"Too often he forgets or neglects to inform me of what's going on. I usually find out as an afterthought or by accident."

"Sometimes he makes decisions in my area without informing me. He 'forgets.'"

B. *Definition.* Employee *trust* was measured by their sense of good faith in interactions, inclusion in operations, caring in relationship, and overall responsibility. Trust creates a productive environment. It allows us to live by positive principles instead of out of fear or a sense of lack. It leads to *good faith,* which allows us to make decisions and take actions in which everyone wins. *Inclusion* is the aspect of trust in which we solicit input and consider how our actions affect others. *Caring* then results in our relationships. This supports an environment of *responsibility* where others need not doubt our word or commitment. Trust was indicated in the survey by such statements as:

"My manager trusts me."
"My manager keeps me fully informed so I feel part of the store."
"My manager relies on me"

C. *Interpretations and Recommendations.* Several of your staff feel that you train well but fail to delegate sufficiently. "He never relaxes. . . . No matter how well I do what he wants, he stays uptight. . . . Why train me if I'm going to be reminded all the time."

When trust is present, it is mutual. Employees will perform even better for you if they sense that you wish to include them in your decisions and will in return act in more inclusive ways. They will share more openly their ideas for store improvement, as well as how they can contribute their talents to the company. You seem to need to learn to let go of the reins with high performers and let them do their best. Are you dragging the top down because of your worries about the bottom? Your team professes to want more inclusion and responsibility. Discuss the accuracy of this and your plan with your manager.

7. OPENNESS

A. *Results.* Your score for this area is 3.42, compared to 3.87 for the Readiserve Group. Your self-assessment was 3.85. Employee comments include the following:

"I'm not saying he deliberately keeps things from me, only that he doesn't always make an effort to communicate."
"I'm not sure that he is aware of everything I need to know. What he does know, he's told me."

B. *Definition.* Openness is necessary to a full and effective flow of communication. We've assessed the openness of the work environment by getting employee feedback on perceived honesty, sharing, communication, and degree of cooperation. Openness results from approaching people and situations without prejudice and unnecessary preconditions. It requires honesty and sharing. *Honesty* means we relate to others free of deception, and *sharing* refers to the accessibility of our experience, lessons and information. *Communication* is the understandable transfer of information, thoughts and feelings, while *cooperation* happens when we interact with others in such a way that our combined efforts are beneficial to all. This principle is reflected in such survey statements as:

"My manager willingly shares relevant and appropriate information with me."
"My manager fosters cooperation among store personnel."

C. *Interpretation and Recommendations.* Results indicate that you need to become more aware of other's need for inclusion. Be mindful of both information they need and things you should hear that you might prefer to avoid. Soliciting feedback and questions is a good way to do more of this. You may also need to listen more by pausing a bit longer before responding to others. This will allow them more air time. Remember, you are an authority figure and most staff will be reticent to speak freely with you.

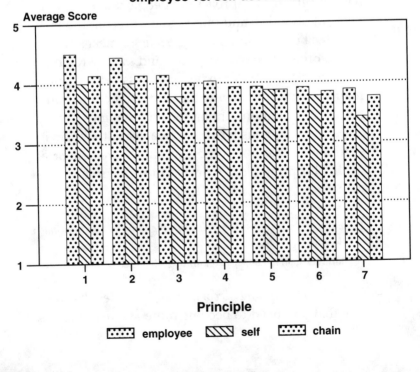

CARMINE
employee vs. self-assessment

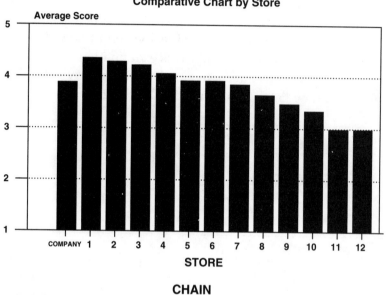

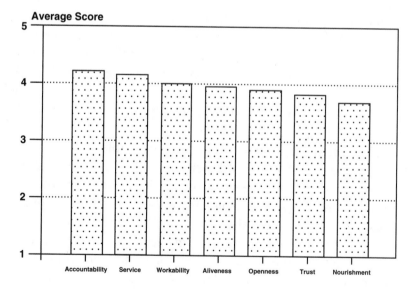

INTERBANK

We saw how in Chapter 9 Ed brought his bank directors together to develop their purpose statement. Once this was devel-

oped, they set up three different flip charts. On the left chart they defined the present state of the bank, listing all the strengths, weaknesses, resources, goals, and problems. On the far right chart, they outlined their ideal vision of how this purpose would manifest in the bank. This examination gave them a foundation to examine alternative pathways for arriving at their ideal, which they listed on the middle flip chart.

Present state	Pathways	Ideal state (vision)

They next discussed the values and principles by which they would achieve their objectives. Here they were outlining their success strategy. This was necessary before developing a strategic plan, because it established the foundation for that plan.

The group generated a long list, which they examined for redundancies. They discussed which principle they would choose if they could choose only one by which to run their business. They discussed the strengths and weaknesses of each principle and how each would ultimately influence corporate problem solving, planning, and operations.

They finally arrived at a list of five principles they thought would guide them in the fulfillment of their corporate purpose. These were excellence, service, responsibility, alignment, and empowerment. These principles were then examined in hypothetical and real business situations they had experienced to see if they provided the guidance the group expected. When they began examining the principles in sales and performance-related compensation situations, they found the list wanting and decided to add accountability to the mix.

Excellence

Service

Responsibility

Alignment

Empowerment

Accountability

They evolved a plan to introduce their purpose and then one principle a month to the bank—this gradual rollout suited them, because they felt they would have the freedom to adjust course and make variations as they went without causing undue confusion in the organization.

For the most effective use of their principles, Ed's group wrote definitions, developed operating assumptions, and articulated standards to guide daily behavior for themselves. They, in effect, were defining purposeful behavior. These were later developed for each employee position in the bank. Without guidelines like these, it is virtually impossible for some people, especially concrete thinkers, to use the principles and purpose optimally and meaningfully. You will notice that the form for each principle varies. This is a reflection of the different executives who presented the new principle each month.

We will now review some of Interbank's introductory documents articulating definitions, operating assumptions, and standards for each of the six principles they found to be essential.

Purpose

"To engage fully and professionally in the creation of financial success for all our constituencies; to provide wealth enhancement and security for clients; financial security along with personal growth and professional achievement for our employees, and exceptional returns on both financial and human capital employed for the shareholders."

Principles

Principles are the dynamic creative element behind how things operate. We have chosen several principles to actualize our purpose. Our success is founded on our ability to focus on these.

Operating Assumption: We assume that if we learn to live in consonance with these principles, we will succeed in our purpose to enhance the well-being and wealth of our clients, our investors, and ourselves.

Standard: We will continually learn to operate in increasingly effective alignment with our principles.

Operating Assumptions

Operating assumptions articulate what we believe or assume will happen when we operate in consonance with any given principle. They help us clarify to what the principle will lead to when applied.

Advantages and Disadvantages of Adopting Principles

Advantages	Disadvantages
Focus	Makes some people uncomfortable
Efficiency	Managers will feel a loss of control
Quality	Change is uncomfortable for some
Client satisfaction	More conflicts in the open
Own satisfaction	Feel excluded
Motivation	
Profit	
Volume	
Fun	
Flat Structure	
More Time To Sell	
Communication	

Operating Assumptions	Standards
We assume that following the path of excellence will put us ahead of our competition.	We will continuously monitor, meet, and exceed the standards of excellence in our industry and our world.
We assume that clients will appreciate and pay more for excellence.	We will solicit and respond to client feedback about our areas of performance.

We assume that setting standards of and measuring excellence will enhance our performance.	Job Performance
	  Appraisal, Setting Objectives, Measuring Performance
	Investment Performance
	  Appraisal, Setting Objectives, Measuring Performance
	Service Excellence
	  Appraisal, Setting Objectives, Measuring Performance
	Marketing and Sales Excellence
	  Appraisal, Setting Objectives, Measuring Performance

Operating Agreements

Operating Agreements are ways we agree to conduct ourselves in the course of doing business. Operating agreements operationalize principles. They take them from the realm of the abstract to the specific. They represent specific intentions.

Standards

Standards refer to the levels of performance to which we orient and below which we do not allow our performance to fall. They are behavioral agreements that take operating agreements into specific areas, duties and expectations.

Excellence

Excellence refers to the state or fact of excelling, the possession chiefly of good qualities in an eminent or unusual degree. We intend excellence in product, in service, in practice, in interaction, in all we do. In order for us to truly know what is excellent, we must use the principles of accountability, responsibility, and service. We must also know what is standard practice and performance outside the Bank in order to establish our benchmark.

Operating Assumptions	*Standards*
We assume that our success will be assured by focusing our efforts on the best customer service possible.	We will constantly monitor customer satisfaction. We will set and adhere to the highest service standards.
We assume that the best in service will lead to our growth.	We will focus on satisfied customers until they refer friends, invest more, and cause growth.
We assume that we must serve each other internally so that we can recreate that experience in our customers.	We agree to do our jobs to the best of our ability. We agree to "go the extra mile" and serve each other as fully as possible.
We assume that a culture of universal service is necessary to deliver the best in service.	We agree to learn to maintain and grow an attitude of service in all we do.
A team that works will make our clients feel we care for them.	We must align with the Bank's mission to make clients feel we have their interests at heart.

Service

Service means to deliver goods or address the needs of another. When we speak of service, we mean to dedicate what we do to the ultimate purpose and well-being of those whom we serve. We refer not only to duty but to an attitude of gratitude and devotion that extends through all we do as we dedicate ourselves to the fulfillment of our customers' higher purposes as well as our own.

Service takes place within the organization as we empower each other to take responsibility and succeed in our stated goals and desires.

Operating Assumptions	Standards
We will generate the greatest possible performance with the highest level of staff responsibility.	We take absolute responsibility for the success of our jobs.
Personal responsibility is key to organizational success, services, alignment, empowerment.	The range of our responsibilities extends to all aspects of the business.
Responsibility is both an attitude and a learned skill.	We will continually strive to learn greater skills in attitude and performance.
100 percent responsibility for bank success can be taken by each employee.	We hold ourselves personally responsible for the Bank's success.
We are better and stronger if staff takes initiative as soon as possible.	Problems are resolved at the lowest possible level. The chain of command is clear.
We have greater chance of success if we concentrate our efforts on the work to be accomplished.	Above all, the staff should strive for excellence, this is the unique reason to become part of the Bank. The Bank serves, supports, and rewards those who serve well and accomplish their work.

Responsibility

Responsibility means answering to something, being morally accountable, being capable of fulfilling an obligation or trust. As a principle, responsibility refers to the 100 percent accountability that each individual assumes for the fulfillment of the Bank's Mission.

· Responsibility understands equally the response to an expectation, the moral needs, of being capable of fulfilling an obligation or earning confidence. Our highest responsibility is to the overall purpose of the bank, which is to enhance the wealth of our depositors, our owners, and ourselves.

Responsibility implies the act of assuming accountability for a job or a need, or of earning confidence.

Alignment

Alignment means to be ordered in parallel toward the same objective. In this case, the principle of alignment refers to the ordering and arrangement of staff around the Bank's higher purpose. We assume that alignment around the Bank's purpose will lead to optimal purpose fulfillment. We agree to align in service to our customers and each other and agree to the greatest good of all. We remain alert to the movement around us and seek to harmonize our activities with the organization at large.

Empowerment

Empowerment refers to our ability to facilitate each other's highest performance through help, communication, challenge, and other means of support. By empowerment, we support each other to do our work more effectively. We create an environment of cooperation and mutual appreciation. We support each other to remain true to the operating principles of the Bank. By following the principle of empowerment, the whole can truly be greater than the sum of its parts.

Operating Assumptions	Standards
Alignment will maximize the results that flow from our efforts.	Staff will seek to align efforts with corporate purpose and principles for the greatest mutual benefit.
All activities in which we engage are to be in the service of the Bank's purpose.	Groups and individuals will maintain awareness of the Bank purpose and be sure to align efforts. We will volunteer to help others meet client needs and tough assignments.
Full and complete information is necessary for proper alignment.	Staff will be given what they need to know for alignment. Bank goals will be freely discussed. Bank progress, performance, and results will be freely discussed.
The success of any one of us is a success for the whole team.	We will celebrate our successes together. We will focus individual effort on harmonious teamwork to enhance alignment and success.

Accountability

Accountability means being liable to be called to account or to answer for responsibilities in conduct or discharge of duties; answerable; responsible; truthful with persons and systems.
To be accountable means:

- to be involved
- to apply oneself
- have a sense of duty
- respect one's own work and the work of others
- desire to progress and succeed

Operating Assumptions	*Standards*
To fulfill its mission the Bank needs to develop every staff member to his or her fullest potential.	Training will be provided to equip everyone with the tools they need.
We are here to help each other get the work done.	We will volunteer to help others meet client needs.
Accepting more responsibilities and challenges assists our personal and professional development.	Those tackling tough assignments will be encouraged and supported.
Immediate and honest feedback helps us to improve performance.	We have a duty of care for each other to provide constructive feedback.
All human beings respond to being valued and appreciated.	We will recognize and reward those who empower others to perform by celebrating their successes.
We can do more as a team than we can as individuals.	We will invest in the success of those around us.

Operating Assumptions	*Standards*
Accountability brings out the best in people and groups by setting and monitoring standards.	Staff will know and receive feedback on performance related to all significant standards.
Accountability supports consciousness and progress.	Staff will discuss performance.
Accountability helps teams coordinate.	Logical discipline without ambiguity. A solid standard both formal and informal, to encourage success. A structure that adapts to need and function. Awareness. Reinforcement.

ACCOUNTABILITY IN SALES

Operating Agreements of All Sales Staff

- establish lists of all contacts and maintain them
- maintain department quality standards in service
- meet quotas for client meetings daily and quarterly
- make timely complete reports on all performances
- make goals for finances and career development personally
- communicate all statistics
- celebrate successes

Quantitative Measures

- number of telephone calls
- number of client visits
- number of active clients
- number of managed accounts
- funds under management
- ratio of deposits to withdrawals

Qualitative Measures

- number of client contacts
- number of referrals
- increased deposits
- number of complaints

CONCLUSION

We have now seen three companies and some of the ways they operationalize their chosen principles of purpose. These are only a few mechanisms we can use to keep ourselves focused and on the path. The possibilities are limited only by our imagination. What matters most is that we practice what we preach and keep fighting the good fight. We must find ways to keep our ideals in front of us as reminders. The more we set up the game of business so we get the best feedback, the more possible and real will be our learning and growing and fulfillment of our individual and corporate purposes.

It is important that corporate principle structures reflect your organization and that you have your corporate purpose in harmony with your life purpose. There will be adjustments on the way. Adventures will happen, problems and opportunities will present themselves. The principles are your tools and guides on the adventure of corporate success and fulfillment.

By focusing on the principles of purpose, your firm will develop the best and most appropriate applications for you. It is important to remember that all tools are founded in principles and that the principles flow from and are tools in themselves to achieve our highest corporate purpose.

The real test to us is our ability to follow through and keep our purpose before us—to create an environment where all play the game together and fully—reaching to be our best and learning to enjoy the never-ending journey toward our highest.

The bottom line is no longer financial capital alone. It has taken a strong turn toward human capital, without which our corporations would have no purpose. We are in a steep evolutionary curve of transformation as we learn the lesson oft repeated by my mentor and business advisor, Virginia Rogers, retired founder and CEO of Cellular One in Chicago, "good business is only good if it is good for all concerned"—customers, owners, employees, humanity, and the environment.

Index

About the Author
and the Opportunities

Bob Wright founded the Living Visions and Vision in Action Corporations to inspire and teach others to live their visions and their dreams, rather than dream their lives. In addition to founding and operating his highly acclaimed national service business for fifteen years, Bob is an internationally recognized author, speaker, educator, consultant and trainer dedicated to helping others live, love, and perform to their fullest.

Over the past eighteen years, Bob has developed the widely respected Comprehensive Personal Development Theory and Model which has guided many to greater success and fulfillment.

Bob believes in the innate power of ability of all. For him, there is no need to wait for the right job or situation. His mission is to help people see and access the possibilities of fulfillment in each and every moment and situation of their lives. He has personally coached most of the people whose stories exemplify the principles in *Beyond Time Management: Business with Purpose,* helping them to face and surmount the obstacles to living their highest vision.

He commits his fullest energies personally to a respectful relationship with the earth, helping individuals live the lives they want in a world that supports them. He is the founder of the Leadership Council for Complex Organizations, with members from the United Sates and Europe; the Men's Guild, a men's organization devoted to developing conscious community leadership; and Be Heard, an environmental awareness and action group.

With his wife Judith, Bob owns and operates The Center, a transformative training and retreat facility near Elkhorn, Wisconsin where individuals and groups can plan and learn the skills needed to make the changes that help them build purposeful lives and businesses. They also bring to focus the Living Spirit Association, which supports members of all faiths in the fullest worship and expression of their highest selves.

He can be contacted at Living Visions Inc.
Suite 260
445 E. Ohio
Chicago, Illinois 60611
Telephone (312) 645-8300
Fax (312) 645-8333

More Information and Tools
for Purpose Development

More Information on the concepts and philosophy of fulfilled responsibility brought forth in *Beyond Time Management* is available through Living Visions. You may subscribe to their quarterly newsletter which chronicles the challenges and victories of those engaged in the development of their highest...

and/or

You can order the workbook and audio tapes to facilitate your purpose development based on the materials from the book.

Complete the following information with $20.00 for the Newsletter and/or $49.95 for the Purpose development workbook and tape to the address on the previous page or telephone your order or fax with a credit card number and expiration to the phone number on the previous page

or

If you just want to be on our mailing list, send only your name and address

Name _____

Address _____

City_____

State _____

Zip _____